Mont Rest Inn
Favorite recipes from our kitchens

Celebrating 21 Years of Great Cooking

Edited by Christine Zraick-Baker

For Copies of this book Contact :
Mont Rest Inn
300 Spring Street
Bellevue, Iowa 52031-1125

Phone number: 563-872-4220
Fax: 563-872-5094
Email: innkeeper@montrest.com

CONTENTS

Recipes

A Wedding Celebration Bouquet at Mont Rest

Chocolate Mousse in a Chocolate Tea Cups

ACKNOWLEDGMENTS

My special thanks and recognition goes to Naomi Kueter. For over a decade she has supervised the training of all the Chefs and Cooks we have here at Mont Rest. Naomi has worked at Mont Rest since she was in high school. Simply put Mont Rest wouldn't be Mont Rest without her.

Among her notable accomplishments, she and her younger brother, Shorty Brunson (currently a chef for Sea Salt in Naples, Florida) prepared a birthday celebration dinner at Mont Rest for Vice President Al Gore and his guests when he ran for President. She has staged hundreds of events including our Famous Murder Mystery dinners, private candlelight celebrations, wine pairing dinners and many weddings banquets.

Thank you Chef Ron Garrett. Your guiding wisdom is priceless.

A salute to pastry Chefs Ruth Kiel and Dolores Huffman. Thanks for keeping us in dough.

Thanks to Dave "the farmer" Gregorich. You can't make a great meal without great fresh ingredients.

I feel fortunate and thankful for our staff members past and present, many who have been employed here at the Inn for years.

Their constant efforts for excellence have made Mont Rest's celebrated service possible.

A special thanks to my oldest daughter, Caryn, for helping compile my recipes into a readable format. Thanks to my daughter Ginny for the initial organization of my array (or should I say disarray) of recipes. Many thanks go to my husband, Ralph, also an author, for all of his support (and proof reading). Also, thank you to my daughter Bridget, who encouraged me to complete this book.

A cordial acknowledgment to my guests that have sent me their family recipes to share with others. Your generous, giving nature shines brightly.

DEDICATION

This Dedication is to remember all the wonderful people that profoundly influenced my joy of cooking and appreciation of good food.

The list is enormous but it particularly includes my Mother, Elaine. It also includes Grandmere Fernande Leone Dubief -Silver, and my Tayta, Mary Zraick, both immigrants to America, who had a vast and deep knowledge that included cooking which lives on in the generations that followed. I would also like to dedicate this volume to my Children and Husband, who love to eat my cooking.

I also dedicate this book to Ruth Nebergall and Shirley Edler who taught me as if I was their own daughter, and to Olivet Werling who helped me understand that food is truly a celebration and not just eating.

This book is also an acknowledgement to Chef Ron Garrett and all the Chefs I've meet over the years here in America and overseas that invited me to into their kitchens to share their knowledge and expertise with me. It is also an expression of appreciation to Dr. Fred Meyer, who has been a wonderful dining partner for my husband and me at many of the most wonderful restaurants and eateries in the United States.

And last, it is dedicated to all the wonderful guests I've had the honor of knowing over the years who have asked for my recipes and for second helpings. Thank you from the depths of my heart.

Chris and her 3 daughters at Naomi's Mont Rest Wedding

INTRODUCTION

Recipes, great food and love bring so much more pleasure when they are shared. I absolutely believe cooking is an act of love. I always laugh when I hear the stories about someone's Great Aunt who took the secret recipe of her special dish with her to her grave. It also makes me a little sad. That person is remembered for her selfish and stingy nature instead of her "joie de vivre" and her wonderful ability to cook. I hope those days are gone.

Food is edible art. It is a rainbow, a sunset, a flower and a kiss. It is here briefly and then it is gone. Luckily for us there is always more. Preparing food is the anticipation of all things joyous and wonderful. It is the moveable feast of life.

For close to three decades Mont Rest has been preparing and serving meals for thousands of wonderful people. They have celebrated every special occasion that you can imagine, from weddings and birthdays to returning soldiers that made it home safely. I feel so grateful they allowed Mont Rest to be a part of it all.

The recipes in this book are a collection of all the celebratory meals that have been shared at my Inn. I have edited them to fit portions for you in your kitchen. May you feel all the beauty and sense of occasion they represent. I feel compelled to quote Julia Childs' most famous phrase: "Bon Appetit".

HISTORY

The historical forces that have influenced the natural beauty that surrounds Mont Rest are in actuality, pre-historic. During the Ice Age, that occurred over 50,000 years ago, the advancing and receding ice flows missed the area that includes Bellevue, sparing the land from the flattening process. Geologists have labelled this region of rolling hills and bluffs as "the Driftless Area". From the air, it looks like an inverted piece of pie.

The Driftless Region of Iowa is thinly populated. As one travels the great River Road, the valleys tumble down to the Mississippi River. Much of the land is virtually wild, with a great deal of it locked up in public hands. The states of Iowa, Illinois, and Wisconsin maintain an extensive number of wildlife management areas in the region for miles surrounding Bellevue, (basically hunting and fishing areas), along with state forests, state parks and wildlife refuges. When you explore the areas around Mont Rest, it is impossible not to realize you are someplace unique and relatively unspoiled.

Day Trip From Galena to Bellevue Circa 1910

Bellevue Midsummer Festival Excursion Circa 1900

HISTORY

It is also unfair to refer to the colorful history of Mont Rest without giving homage to Bellevue's historic connections to Galena, Illinois. Bellevue is one of the oldest towns west of the Mississippi because it was the frontier "sister city" to this powerhouse town. At one time, Galena was three times larger in population than Chicago. It was the home to nine Civil War generals, including Ulysses S. Grant, and many of the Riverboat Pilots for the Mississippi. There were daily excursion boats from the Port of Galena in the Fever River to the Port of Bellevue. U. S. Grant, for instance, would often come to Bellevue to sell tanned leather skins to a bootery, Lucke Brothers, in downtown Bellevue.

Leaving Downtown Bellevue

To Board a Paddle Wheeler

Circa 1925

"In the Good Old Summer Time" Bellevue, IA

During the late 1800's the Mississippi River was overflowing with passenger and cargo paddle wheelers. It was the equivalent of an interstate highway. At night it was difficult to see anything of interest on shore, therefore many travelers would sit down in the dining room after dinner for a friendly game of poker. They, of course, became easy prey for "Riverboat Dandies", professional gamblers in fancy garb, complete with French ruffled shirts, just waiting to get less experienced poker players into a game of chance.

As you will read, Seth Luellyn Baker didn't want to have to take a boat ride to gamble. He built Mont Rest in 1893 for $6,000.

HISTORY

The Stern Wheeler, The Sidney, Landing at Bellevue

Packet Boats Carried Cargo Along The Mississippi

HISTORY

The Mississippi from McGregor Heights, Iowa

Driveway to Mont Rest 1911

HISTORY

Mont Rest was built in 1893 for $6,000 by Seth Luellyn Baker. He was a wealthy land developer who owned hotels, gold mines and packet boats on the Mississippi. Baker was a true entrepreneur. He developed the town of Glen Ellyn, Illinois, and he loved to gamble. Seth Baker was originally from Bellevue and came back to buy what was known as the north bluff of Bellevue. As so many newly rich Victorians, he erected a monument to his stature in life. He named the property Mont Rest. The locals almost immediately started calling Mont Rest "The Castle" because of its unusual architecture and its towering presence over the town.

Baker built the round room at the top of the house for high stake poker games. Professional gamblers used to ride the steam paddle wheelers from points south of St. Louis just to get into gambling games in the tower at Mont Rest. You had to be a high roller just to be invited to these high stake games.

Several local farms exchanged hands late at night in the round room at the top of Bellevue's Castle. The gamblers would walk up an inside stairwell, climb through a hatch, step out onto the roof of the house, to gain entrance to the gambling room. They could barricade themselves up there for days with no threat from local law enforcement officials. Gambling was illegal on the shores in those days. Mont Rest soon became infamous for its gambling.

MONT REST 1893

HISTORY

In 1895 a doctor of questionable credentials from St. Louis, Missouri called a hand in a poker game with a $6,000 bet. Mr. Baker thought he could beat this man's hand, and being short of cash offered the deed to his beloved Mont Rest to call the bet. The man accepted and the cards were laid down. Baker then proceeded to go downstairs and tell his wife that they had two weeks to move out. In 1895 $6,000 in cash was the buying equivalent of in excess of 2 million dollars today.

The doctor who won the hand only lived in Mont Rest for a couple of years, seeing patients intermittently and treating all sorts of illness with mild electrical shock treatments. Doc sold the house, and the house was sold again to a nationally prominent figure named Frank Weinshenk who was a business partner of Henry Ford.

Mr. Weinshenk spent his life and his fortune trying to get a telephone line established before WWI between Mont Rest and the Pope in Rome. He went as far as trying to sue Bell Telephone Systems for "persecution of religion" because they would not honor his request to lay a trans-Atlantic cable on the ocean floor starting in Bellevue and stretching to the Vatican.

Residence of Frank Weinschenk Circa 1939

HISTORY

Frank Weinschenk

HISTORY

After Weinshenk the house went to a series of owners, including a priest, until it became owned by a man who employed 200 people in a factory located in Bellevue and lived in Mont Rest like a king.

However, the man became very upset about a rumor that was going around the gossip mills in town and shut the house up as a punishment to the town.

He refused to sell it anyone for a quarter of a century. The forest behind Mont Rest encroached the property. Animals began living in Mont Rest and teenagers broke the windows. The house became known as the Haunted Castle of Bellevue. In 1979 The Des Moines Register ran an article about the Haunted Castle of Bellevue and how it stood brooding over the north bluff of Bellevue.

Mont Rest Vacant for 25 years Circa 1979

HISTORY

In the early 80's, the gentlemen who had held onto the house for a quarter of a century finally sold it to another gentlemen who was going to renovate the house and live there in his retirement. He soon realized that maintenance of a mansion was going to occupy more time than he desired, so he sold it to a young couple who started a remodeling job. They however, faced financial ruin and gave the house back to the bank. At which time the present owner, Christine Zraick-Baker purchased the property from the local bank and started the long trek to its total restoration.

She opened up the residence as a Country Inn and it soon became very famous for its beautiful, peaceful views of the Mississippi River, and the fun parties the innkeeper would throw centering around murder mystery plots. Christine who had opened up Iowa's first bed and breakfast inn in her home town, now acquired Mont Rest as her second endeavor in 1986.

Mont Rest - Early 1990's

HISTORY

In 1996 on Christmas Eve, Mont Rest was almost totally destroyed in a tremendous fire. They called in five fire stations in which an excess of fifty firemen battled the blaze all night, dumping over 650,000 gallons of water on the structure. Emotionally devastated, Christine was not sure whether Mont Rest could be rebuilt. Her ten year dream had gone up in smoke, but due to the overwhelming response from the people of Bellevue and her own feelings of stewardship towards the property, she decided in the Spring of 1997 at least to try to recreate what had been standing there for over a century.

Christmas Eve Fire 1996

Fire Damage - Parlor

Fire Damage - Upstairs

HISTORY

Today Mont Rest is back in all its Victorian splendor. Everything that the fire had destroyed has been replaced with vintage woodwork, chandeliers, and antique furniture that I literally searched the world to find. One of my biggest joys is sharing this Victorian wonder with my guests.

June 2010

MURDER MYSTERIES

Mont Rest's Murder Mysteries have a rich history that started before Mont Rest Inn even existed. I started them at the mansion I owned, Victorian House Bed and Breakfast, located in my home town of Tipton, Iowa.

I grew up next to the mansion on what was known as "Tipton's Boulevard", East Fourth Street. In 1979 I was living and working near Lincoln Park on the near north side of Chicago when that grand mansion in Tipton was going up for auction. It was in jeopardy of being torn down to make way for many new houses. I bought it, fixed it up, and got it placed on the National Register of Historic Places. I opened it as Iowa's first Bed and Breakfast and started my Murder Mysteries there in the early 1980's. I sold it to a couple from California in 1989. They sold it in the mid-ninties to a family as a private residence today. I moved my murder mysteries and my family to the new location, Mont Rest, and have been doing over 100 murder mysteries every year since. The wonderful food is a large part of the experience and many of our entrees in this book are served during our Mystery nights.

Listed below is an outline of our Murder Mysteries parties as they exist today:

You become a character in an intriguing Agatha Christie-type plot and solve a spine-tingling "who-done-it"

You receive a character outline. We fully costume you , head to toe , to immerse you into the character that you become. We start you with a sumptuous hors d'oeuvre party where you mingle with other "suspects". We serve you a gourmet dinner, drinks, and dessert while you try to figure out " who did it".

Murder Mysteries are hosted typically every weekend all year round. Your evening begins at 5:30 and ends at approximately 9:30.

Come dressed casually because we will costume you from head to toe.

We guarantee the removal of dead bodies!

THE INN TODAY

In 2011 Mont Rest is celebrating 25 years as a Bed and Breakfast Inn. Today we entertain people from all over the world. We have become a destination for special occasions that are in tune with the demands of discerning travelers. Our inn also serves as a reminder of how things were over 100 years ago.

From the moment you walk through the door, Mont Rest transports you back to a lost era of grace and beauty. This historic Inn is Iowa's most luxurious bed and breakfast. Fully restored since the fire on Christmas Eve 1996, Mont Rest is nestled halfway up a 9 acre wooded bluff overlooking one of the most panoramic views of the mighty Mississippi River. Many people love to sit in a rocker on the front porch and watch eagles catching fish from the Mississippi.

We're the perfect setting for a honeymoon, anniversary, or just a weekend getaway offering a luxurious alternative to cookie cutter motels and hotels. We offer twelve luxurious guest rooms with private baths.

THE INN TODAY

All of our luxury rooms feature working fireplaces, King and Queen-sized beds, Jacuzzi whirlpool bathtubs, cable TV with DVD players, heated towel bars, Egyptian cotton towels, guest robes, hair dryers, and handmade chocolates. Complimentary non-alcoholic beverages are available in our main floor guest kitchen.

The inn offers such Spa services as in-room therapeutic massage and reflexology, manicures, and pedicures. Our concierge service includes reserving tee times at the Bellevue Golf Club, arranging dinner river cruises, booking canoe trips, making dinner reservations for area restaurants, getting tickets to local sporting and theater events in the surrounding area, and providing other information on tourist- related activities. Mont Rest is close to several large gaming facilities and ski resorts. I believe the services provided for our guests during their stay by our staff are top drawer.

When you stay here you will awake to the smell of fresh baked cinnamon rolls and pastries, French press coffee and Chai tea. Just ask anyone who has ever stayed here about their fondest memories...

We look forward to seeing you.

AN INN FOR ALL SEASONS

Spring on the bluff brings a lime green color to the budding trees

Springtime view from the Bellevue Room

AN INN FOR ALL SEASONS

The waters and skies become sapphire blue as Spring gives way to early Summer

What a great day to have a picnic on the water

AN INN FOR ALL SEASONS

Late Summer explodes with color at Mont Rest

AN INN FOR ALL SEASONS

Fall is a great time to snuggle in bed watching the leaves change color

AN INN FOR ALL SEASONS

A Victorian Christmas is nothing short of wonderous

Eagles sit by the dozens in Winter garding the
bluffs behind Bellevue's Castle

RECIPES

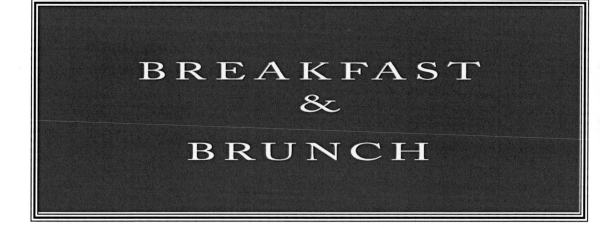

BREAKFAST
&
BRUNCH

Breakfast Quiche Page 28

BREAKFAST & BRUNCH

Tomato Basil Frittata

Yields 2 Servings

3/4 teaspoons	Olive Oil
1/4 cup	Green onions - chopped
1 medium	Tomato - diced
1 Tablespoons	Fresh Basil - chopped
4	Eggs
1/4 teaspoon	Pepper

Heat oil in a nonstick skillet. Sauté onions for one minute and stir in tomato and basil. Heat thoroughly. In a medium bowl beat eggs thoroughly and add pepper. Pour over tomato onion mixture. As the mixture begins to set lift the cooked portion so the uncooked portion and flow to the bottom. Try to avoid stirring. Cook 4 to 5 minutes or until eggs are cooked thoroughly. Top with mozzarella cheese.

BREAKFAST & BRUNCH

Breakfast Strata

Yields 8 Servings

8	Slices of Bread, crusts removed
14	Eggs
3/4 cup	Heavy Cream
1 teaspoon	Garlic Powder
1 teaspoon	Salt
½ teaspoon	Pepper
1 ¼ cup	Shredded Cheese, reserve ¼ cup
3/4 cup	Shredded Mozzarella Cheese, reserve ¼ cup
1/2 cup	Diced Cured Ham
1/4 cup	Green Pepper, chopped
1/4 cup	Red Onion, chopped
1/2 cup	Mushrooms, sliced
1/2 cup	Butter

Sauté onions, peppers, and mushrooms in butter. The last 2 minutes add ham. Set aside. In a large bowl beat eggs and cream together, add garlic powder, salt, and pepper, mix well. 9x14 pan. Spray well. Arrange bread in bottom of pan. Sprinkle shredded cheese and shredded mozzarella cheese on bread. Add sauteed onions, peppers, mushrooms, and ham. Pour egg mixture and top with remaining cheese. Dust with Dill Weed and Paprika. Let sit for 5 minutes. Bake at 350 degrees for 45 minutes to 1 hour. May garnish with more paprika and dill weed.

BREAKFAST & BRUNCH

Rice Porridge

Yields 4 Servings

4 cups	Cooked Wild White Rice Mix
1/2 cup	Pure Maple Syrup (plus more for serving)
2 tablespoons	Butter
1/4 cup	Dried Blueberries or Raisins
1/4 cup	Craisins, and Dried Cherries
1/2 cup	Roasted Cracked Hazelnuts or Pecans
1 ½ cup	Heavy Cream plus more, warmed, for serving

In a heavy non-stick sauté pan, add cooked rice, butter, heavy cream, and maple syrup, and warm through. Add the blueberries, craisins, cherries, and hazelnuts. Stir to mix well. Serve in a bowl with sides of warm heavy cream and maple syrup.

Belgian Waffles Page 26

Belgian Waffles

Yields 4 Servings

1 cup, 2 tablespoons	Jiffy Mix
3 tablespoons	Sugar
1 cup	Milk
2	Eggs
1/2 cup	Butter, melted
1 teaspoon	Vanilla

In a medium bowl combine Jiffy mix and sugar. Combine egg yolks and milk and add to Jiffy mixture, mix until smooth. Stir in butter. In a separate bowl beat egg whites until peaks form. Fold in to batter. Add vanilla and stir.

Waffle Topping

5 Tablespoons	Butter, softened
1 cup	Powdered Sugar
1 1/2 cup	Whipped Cream
1 lb	Strawberries, sliced

Mix butter and sugar well. Keep refrigerated. When ready to serve soften powdered sugar mixture and stir in whipped cream. Drizzle over warm waffle and top with fresh sliced strawberries and whipped cream. Garnish with a fanned strawberry.

BREAKFAST & BRUNCH

Sunday Brunch
Breakfast Potatoes

Yields 4 Servings

¼ cup	Onions, diced
4 tablespoons	Butter
¼ cup	Corn Oil
1 16 bag	Hashbrowns
¼ teaspoon	Garlic Salt
¼ teaspoon	Pepper
¼ teaspoon	Poultry Seasoning

In large pan over medium heat, melt butter and oil. Add onions and cook until translucent, approximately 5 minutes. Add shredded potatoes and seasoning. Cook for 5-10 minutes until the potatoes begins to brown. Flipping one to two times during the cooking process. Be sure not over work the potatoes. Add additional oil and butter if needed. Garnish with fresh parsley. **Variations:** Home Fries: Boil potatoes until a fork comes out easily. Slice into 1/8 inch slices. Cook the same as the hash browns. Garnish with fresh parsley.

BREAKFAST & BRUNCH

Breakfast Quiche

Yields 6-8 Servings

1	9-inch pie shell, deep dish
9	Eggs
1/2 cup	Heavy Cream
1 teaspoon	Garlic Powder
1 teaspoon	Salt
1/2 teaspoon	Pepper
1 cup	Swiss Cheese, cubed
1/2 cup, 1/4 cup	Shredded Mozzarella Cheese
1/4 cup	Green Pepper, chopped
1/4 cup	Onion, chopped
1/2 cup	Mushrooms, sliced
1/4 cup	Butter
1/2 teaspoon	Paprika
1/2 teaspoon	Dill Weed

Sauté onions, peppers, and mushrooms in butter. Set aside. In a large bowl beat eggs and milk together, add garlic powder, salt, and pepper, mix well. Sprinkle 1/2 cup mozzarella cheese and 1 cup swiss cheese in bottom for pie shell. Add onion and mushroom mixture. Pour egg mixture in shell and top with remaining cheese. Bake at 350 degrees for 1 hour. Garnish with paprika and dill weed.

BREAKFAST & BRUNCH

Country Style Ham in a Clove Reduction Sauce

Yields 8 Servings

8 large slices	Boneless Ham, sliced one inch
4 tablespoons	Butter
½ cup	Brown Sugar
½ cup	Pineapple Juice
¼ teaspoon	Ground Cloves

In small heavy saucepan over medium heat, melt butter. When butter is melted add brown sugar and pineapple juice. Cook for 5-10 minutes or until the sauce begins to thicken. Add ham coating both sides. Cook until heated thoroughly. Place into a serving dish and top with glaze.

BREAKFAST & BRUNCH

Egg in Puff Pastry

Yields 6 Servings

6	Puff Pastry Squares 5x5x1/8
6	Large Eggs
6 Tablespoons	Shredded Mozzarella Cheese
6 Tablespoons	Shredded Cheddar Cheese
1 cup	Heavy Cream
¼ teaspoon	Salt
¼ teaspoon	Pepper
1/4 teaspoon	Garlic Powder
3/4 teaspoon	Dill Weed
3/4 teaspoon	Paprika

Place thawed puff pastry in large muffin cup, greased. Add 1 tablespoon of shredded mozzarella cheese. Break 1 egg over cheese, keeping the egg whole. Add heavy cream just enough to cover the egg, keeping the egg yolk in the center of the puff pastry. Add a dash of salt, pepper, and garlic powder. Add 1 tablespoon of shredded cheddar cheese and sprinkle dill weed on top of each puff pastry. Bake 350 degrees for 40 minutes or until lightly browned. Serve immediately and garnish with paprika.

Breakfast
Quiche

Page 28

BREAKFAST & BRUNCH

Eggs Poached in Cream

Yields 4 Servings

4 Tablespoons	Butter
6	Eggs
1 cup	Heavy Cream
1/2 teaspoon	Salt
1/2 teaspoon	Pepper
1/2 teaspoon	Paprika

In heavy saucepan over medium heat, melt butter. When butter is melted and hot drop eggs in whole, one at a time. Add heavy cream and salt and pepper to taste. Cook covered for 10 minutes on low. Shut off heat and let rest for 10 minutes. Egg yolks should be cooked thoroughly. Spoon into a serving dish. Garnish with paprika. This was my mother's recipe. Try it and you'll be hooked.

2009 The Twilight Swain heading South to the main channel

Hot Chocolate

Yields 20 Servings

1 cup	Cocoa Powder
2 cup	Powdered Sugar
2 cups	Powdered Milk
1 teaspoon	Salt
2 teaspoons	Cornstarch
1 pinch	Cayenne Pepper

Combine all ingredients well. Storage in an airtight container.

To prepare one serving: Add 3 tablespoons of mix to 6 ounces of hot water. Stir well and serve with whipped topping. Garnish with chocolate shavings.

Ed's New Energy Shake

Yields 4 Servings

1 cup	Cranberry Juice
1 cup	Soy Milk
1 bag	Whole Frozen Strawberries
1 lg.	Banana
1 carton	Egg Beaters (partially thawed)
1 Large	Fresh Strawberry (for garnish)

Mix all ingredients in blender. Serve with fresh strawberries. May also substitute frozen strawberries with mixed frozen fruit.

BREAKFAST & BRUNCH

French Vanilla Cappuccino Mix

Yields 15 Servings

1 cup	Instant Coffee Creamer
1 cup	French Vanilla Coffee Creamer
2/3 cup	Instant Coffee
1/2 cup	Sugar
1/2 teaspoon	Cinnamon
1/4 teaspoon	Nutmeg

Place all ingredients into a blender and blend for a short time.

Storage in an airtight container.

To prepare one serving: Add 3 tablespoons of mix to 6 ounces of hot water. Stir well and serve with whipped topping. Garnish with chocolate shavings.

BREAKFAST & BRUNCH

Chai Tea

Yields 20 Servings

1 cup	Non Fat Powdered Milk
1 cup	French Vanilla Flavored Creamer
2 cups	Granulated Sugar
1 cup	Unsweetened Instant Tea
2 teaspoons	Ground Ginger
2 teaspoons	Ground Cinnamon
1 teaspoons	Ground Cloves
1 teaspoons	Ground Cardamon

Combine all ingredients in a mixer. Blend well. Storage in an airtight container.

To prepare one serving:
Add 3 tablespoons of mix to 6 ounces of hot water. Stir well.

MUFFINS
&
BREADS

Coffee Cake, Sour Cream Banana Muffins, and French Bread

Pages 37, 49, 50, 45

MUFFINS & BREADS

Apple Coffee Cake with Pecans

Yields 15 Servings

3 to 4 cups	Apples
2 teaspoons	Cinnamon
1 1/2 cups divided	Sugar
3 cups	Flour
4 teaspoons	Baking Powder
1 teaspoon	Salt
1 1/2 cups	Milk
3 Large	Eggs
1/2 cup & 2 tablespoons	Melted Butter
1/4 cup	Chopped Pecans
1/4 cup	Brown Sugar
2 Tablespoons	Powdered Sugar

Preheat oven to 350 degrees and grease a 9x13 pan. Slice apples with the skin on into thin wedges. In a large frying pan mix apples with cinnamon and ¾ cups of the sugar. Cook until apples are tender. Set aside. In a large bowl mix together the flour, the rest of the sugar, baking powder, salt, milk, egg, and butter. Pour half of the flour mixture into the 9x13 pan, top with half of the apple mixture and repeat. Mix pecans and brown sugar together, and sprinkle over top. Take the rest of the melted butter and drizzle over the dish. Bake for 50 minutes or until a toothpick inserted in the center comes out clean. Cool for 15 minutes, dust with powdered sugar and serve.

MUFFINS & BREADS

Banana Bread

Yields 1 Loaf

2	Bananas, mashed
¼ cup	Vegetable oil
¼ cup	Butter, melted
¾ cup	Granulated Sugar
¾ cup	Brown Sugar
2	Eggs
1/2 teaspoon	Salt
1/4 cup	Buttermilk or Heavy Cream
1 teaspoon	Vanilla
1 3/4 cup	Flour
1 teaspoon	Baking Soda
¼ teaspoon	Ginger, Nutmeg
1 teaspoon	Cinnamon
1 cup	Pecans

Topping

¼ cup	Pecans
¼ cup	Flour
¼ teaspoon	Cinnamon
2 Tablespoon	Butter, melted

Preheat oven to 325 degrees. Combine bananas, oil, butter, and sugars together. Mix in eggs, milk, and vanilla until incorporated. Stir in flour, soda, salt, and nuts until blended. In a separate bowl, combine Topping ingredients. Pour in a loaf pan, sprinkle topping oven then bake for 1 hour.

MUFFINS & BREADS

Blueberry Bread

Yields 1 Loaf

1/2 cup	Butter
1 1/4 cups	Sugar
3	Eggs
3/4 cup	Milk
2 1/2 cups	Flour
2 teaspoons	Baking Powder
2 cups	Blueberries

Preheat oven to 350 degrees. Cream shortening, sugar, and eggs. Add flour, baking powder, and milk, mix well. Stir in blueberries, pour into loaf pan. Bake at 350 degrees for 45 minutes.

MUFFINS & BREADS

Cappuccino Muffins
Yields 12 servings

Espresso Frosting

4 ounces	Cream Cheese
1 Tablespoon	Sugar
1/2 teaspoon	Instant Coffee Granules
1/2 teaspoon	Vanilla
1/4 cup	Mini Chocolate Chips

Combine all spread ingredients until well blended and refrigerate.

Muffin Mix

2 cups	Flour
3/4 cup	Sugar
2 1/2 teaspoons	Baking Powder
1 teaspoon	Cinnamon
1/2 teaspoon	Salt
1 cup	Milk
1	Egg
1 teaspoon	Vanilla
3/4 cup	Chocolate Chips
2 Tablespoon	Instant Coffee Granules
1/2 cup	Melted Butter

In a small bowl combine flour, sugar, baking powder, cinnamon, and salt. In a medium mixing bowl stir milk and coffee granules until dissolved. Add butter, egg, and vanilla. Stir in dry ingredients and fold in chocolate chips. Grease or line muffin tins. Bake at 375 degrees for 15-20 minutes. Cool for 5 minutes and remove from tins. Spread Espresso Frosting on top of muffins.

MUFFINS & BREADS

Cheddar Bay Biscuits

Yields 12 Servings

2 cups	Baking Mix (like Bisquick)
4 tablespoons	Cold salted butter
3/4 cup	Whole milk (cold)
1 cup	Sharp cheddar cheese, grated (we use 5 yr aged Wisconsin cheddar)
1/2 cup	Butter, melted
3/4 teaspoon	Garlic powder, divided
1 teaspoon	Parsley flakes, divided
1/4 teaspoon	Salt

Preheat oven to 400°F. Combine Bisquick and cold butter. Don't combine too thoroughly. There should be small chunks of butter about the size of peas. Add cheddar, milk, 1/4 teaspoon garlic and a dash of salt. Mix by hand until combined, don't over mix. Drop 9-12 equal portions onto greased cookie sheet or muffin pan. Bake for 15 minutes or until tops are light golden brown. Stir in 1/2 teaspoon garlic powder and 1/2 teaspoon parsley flakes with 1/2 cup melted butter. Use a pastry brush to spread garlic butter over tops of biscuits. Sprinkle salt and 1/2 teaspoon parsley on tops of biscuits.

MUFFINS & BREADS

Chocolate Chip Walnut Loaf

Yields 1 loaf

1 cup	Flour
1 teaspoon	Baking Powder
1/4 cup	Cornstarch
1/2 cup	Softened Butter
2 large	Eggs (beaten)
1 teaspoon	Vanilla
1/4 cup	Walnuts (finely chopped)
1/2 cup	Chocolate Chips
1 teaspoon	Lemon Zest
1 1/2 Tablespoons	Sugar

Preheat oven to 350 degrees. Grease 8 1/2 X 4 1/2 in loaf pan, sprinkle with 1 1/2 Tablespoons of sugar. Sift flour, baking powder, and cornstarch into a mixing bowl, set aside. With an electric mixer, cream butter until soft. Add sugar, and beat until light and fluffy. Add eggs one at a time, beating after each one. Gently fold in dry ingredients into butter mixture, add vanilla, nuts, lemon zest, and chocolate chips. Pour into pan and bake for 45 to 50 minutes.

MUFFINS & BREADS

Cinnamon Rolls
with Cream Cheese Frosting
Yields 12 Dozen

4 -5 cups	Flour
2 packages	Active Dry Yeast
1 teaspoon	Salt
3/4 cup	Milk (Luke warm)
1/2 cup	Water
1/2 cup	Butter (melted)
1/2 cup	Sugar
1	Egg

In a large mixing bowl stir together 1 3/4 cup flour, yeast, and salt, set aside In a small pan heat water, milk, butter, and sugar until very warm (120 - 130 degrees). Add liquid to flour mixture and beat until smooth approximately 2 minutes. Gradually add enough flour to make a soft dough, not sticky. Turn on to a floured surface and knead until smooth and elastic approximately 5 minutes. Cover and let rest 20 to 30 minutes. Roll dough in to a 9x13 sheet. Brush with melted butter. Combine 3 tablespoons of cinnamon with 1 cup of sugar. Spread sugar mixture evenly. Starting with longest side roll evenly in to a jelly roll style. With a sharp knife cut in to 12 equal pieces. Place in greased pan and cover. Let rise for approximately one hour. Bake at 350 degrees until golden brown. Cool for 10 minutes and frost.

Cream Cheese Frosting

1/2 cup	Butter, softened
8 ounces	Cream Cheese
1/3 cup	Milk
2 cup	Powdered Sugar
1 teaspoon	Vanilla

In a large mixing bowl beat butter, and cream cheese. Add powdered sugar, vanilla, and milk. Beat well.

MUFFINS & BREADS

Dinner Rolls

Yields 2 Dozen

1 package	Yeast
1/2 cup plus 1 tablespoon	Sugar
1 cup	Water
1/2 cup	Butter
5 cups	Flour
3 large	Eggs

Preheat oven to 350 degrees. Mix together 1 package of yeast and 1 Table-spoon sugar. Beat in 3 eggs and 1 cup lukewarm water. Let stand for 15 minutes. Add 1/2 cup sugar, 1/2 cup butter (softened), and 1 teaspoon salt. Mix in 5 cups (mix one cup at a time it may not take all 5 cups) of flour, knead well. Let raise for 1 hour and push down. Shape in to rolls. Place in greased baking dish. Cover and let raise for 1 hour. Bake for 15 minutes.

Sour Cream Banana and Great Morning Muffins Pages 50, 46

MUFFINS & BREADS

French Bread

Yields 4 Loaves

3 packages	Yeast (6 ¾ teaspoons)
2 tablespoons	Sugar
4 cups	Warm Water
	(115 degrees – about 2 min. 20 sec in microwave)
2 tablespoons	Salt
9 ½ cups	Flour
2-3 tablespoons	Yellow Corn Meal
1	Egg White
1 tablespoon	Cold Water

Combine yeast with sugar and warm water in a large bowl; stir to dissolve. Mix salt with the flour and add to the yeast mixture. Knead dough, adding flour if necessary. Grease a separate large bowl and place dough seam side down. Cover and let rise in a warm place until doubled in size about 45 minutes to 1 hour. Punch the dough down and cut into four equal portions. Shape into four loaves/rounds and place on a cornmeal-sprinkled baking sheet. Mix egg white with cold water in a small bowl. Slash the tops of loaves on the diagonal with a sharp knife and brush with egg white wash. Place in cold oven, set oven at 400 degrees and bake 35 minutes or until well browned.

Variation

Tomato Basil Boule - shape in to rounds and work in garlic salt, basil, and sun dried tomatoes. Do not leave tomatoes exposed on the top of the loaf. They will burn during baking. Slash on the diagonal. Brush with butter and sprinkle with garlic salt and basil.

MUFFINS & BREADS

Great Morning Muffins

Yields 2 Dozen

1 cup	Carrot Pulp from juicer
Or 1 cup	Apple sauce
2 large	Eggs
2 large	Egg Whites
8 tablespoons	Butter, melted
¾ cup	Corn Oil
4 cups	Flour
1 cup	Chopped Apple
1 cup	Shredded Carrot
½ cup	Raisins
½ cup	Golden Raisins
¼ cup	Dried Cranberries
3 cups	Milk
2 tablespoons	Baking Powder
1 teaspoons	Salt

Cream shortening, sugar, and eggs. Add the remaining ingredients, mix well. Pour into greased muffin cups and bake at 350 degrees for 35 minutes or until done.

MUFFINS & BREADS

Orange Cranberry Scones

Yields 6 scones

1 cup	Self-rising Flour (sifted)
½ teaspoon	Salt
½ cup	Cranberries
1 teaspoon	Orange Juice
2 teaspoons	Orange Zest
3 tablespoons	Lard or Vegetable Fat
2 tablespoons	Sugar
1 (large)	Egg

Milk (A small amount to make the mixture sticky)

In a large bowl add lard to flour and salt. Mix with your hands or fork. Add sugar and cranberries. In a medium bowl whisk egg and milk. Add most of egg mixture (reserve enough to brush on tops of scones). Mix until the dough becomes firm with hands, shape into a ball. Roll flat about 1 inch thick and cut into desired shapes. Place on a parchment lined cooking sheet. Brush tops with remaining egg mixture. Bake at 400 degrees until golden brown about 10 minutes.

MUFFINS & BREADS

Rhubarb Bread

Yields 2 Loaf

3 cups	Brown Sugar
3	Eggs
2 teaspoons	Baking Soda
1/4 teaspoon	Salt
1/2 cup	Nuts
1 teaspoon	Vanilla
3 cups	Rhubarb - chopped
1 1/3 cups	Oil
2 cups	Buttermilk
5 1/4 cups	Flour

In a large mixing bowl mix all ingredients together. Pour into 3 greased bread pans. Bake at 350 degrees for 1 hour. Garnish with cinnamon brown sugar or powdered sugar.

MUFFINS & BREADS

Rhubarb Coffee Cake

Yields 8 Servings

1 ½ cups	Packed Brown Sugar
2/3 cup	Corn Oil
1	Eggs
1 teaspoons	Vanilla
2 ½ cups	Flour
1 teaspoon	Salt
1 teaspoon	Baking Soda
1 cup	Milk
1 1/2 cup	Chopped Rhubarb

In a large bowl, beat brown sugar, oil, egg, and vanilla. Combine flour, salt, baking soda. Add to egg mixture. Beat until smooth. Stir in rhubarb. Pour in to prepared 8" round pan.

Crumb Topping

1/3 cup	Granulated Sugar
1 Tablespoon	Butter, melted
1/3 cup	Pecans, or Almonds

In a small bowl, combine granulated sugar, butter, and nuts. Sprinkle with reserved crumb mixture. Optional add 3/4 cup toasted almonds. Bake at 350 degrees for 35 minutes.

Sour Cream Banana Bread

Yields 1 Loaf

½ cup	Butter, melted
1 cup	Granulated Sugar
2	Eggs
1 teaspoon	Vanilla
1 teaspoon	Almond Extract
1 ½ cups	Flour
1/2 teaspoon	Salt
1 teaspoon	Baking Soda
2	Bananas, mashed
½ cup	Sour Cream
½ cup	Walnuts or Pecans

Topping

¼ cup	Walnuts or Pecans
½ cup	Flour
½ cup	Brown Sugar
¼ cup	Butter, softened

In a large bowl, stir butter and sugar together. Add eggs and vanilla, mix well. Stir in flour, soda, and salt. Fold in sour cream, nuts, and bananas. Pour in a loaf pan, sprinkle topping and Bake at 350 degrees for 1 hour.

APPETIZERS

Baked Brie Page 60

Stuffed Mushroom Caps

Yields 10 Servings

30	Mushrooms
½ cup	Red Onion, diced
2 teaspoons	Minced Garlic
½ teaspoon	Fine Sea Salt
½ teaspoon	White Pepper
½ cup	Parsley, snipped
2 - 8 ounce sticks	Butter, divided
2 cups	Bread Crumbs
¼ cup	Parmesan Cheese
1 cup	Shredded Mozzarella Cheese

Separate mushroom caps and dice stems. Saute diced mushroom stems, onions, garlic in 8 ounces of butter. Combine bread crumbs, parsley, parmesan cheese, shredded mozzarella, salt, and pepper and add to sauted mixture. Fill mushroom caps.

Bake at 350 degrees for 20 minutes. Drizzle with remaining melted butter and garnish with fresh parsley.

APPETIZERS

Caramel Apple Dip

Yields 12 Servings

16 ounces	Cream Cheese, softened
3/4 cup - 1 cup	Brown Sugar
1 teaspoon	Real Vanilla Extract
4	Apples

1 pound of Strawberries (washed with tops still on.)

In a medium mixing bowl mix cream cheese, vanilla, and slowly add brown sugar to color. The cream cheese mixture will have a rich caramel color. Serve with apple wedges or large strawberries.

Taco Dip

Yields 12 Servings

8 ounce package	Cream Cheese
8 ounce container	Sour Cream
1 package	Dry Taco Mix
12 ounce jar	Taco Sauce
2 cups	Chopped Lettuce
1 cup	Tomatoes
2 cups	Shredded Cheddar Cheese

Mix cream cheese, sour cream, and taco mix together, then spread onto cookie sheet. Spread taco sauce over cream cheese mixture. Top with lettuce, tomatoes, and cheese. Chill for several hour and serve with nacho chips.

Cute Baby Shower Buffet Featuring Taco Dip

Crab Dip

Yields 12 Servings

Cream Cheese Mixture

8 ounce	Cream Cheese, softened
6 ounce can	Crab meat, drained or
	6 ounces fresh shredded crab meat
1 ounce	Fresh squeezed lemon juice
1/2 teaspoon	Lemon Zest

Mix all ingredients together with a fork and place in a medium sized serving dish.

Cocktail Sauce

1 cup	Ketchup
1 Tablespoon	Horseradish
¼ teaspoon	Worcestershire Sauce

In a small bowl mix ketchup, horseradish, and worcestershire sauce together Spread on top of the crab mixture and garnish with a lemon twist and parsley curls. Serve with water crackers.

Spinach Dip

Yields 12 Servings

10 ounces frozen	Spinach, chopped, thawed, and drained
8 ounces can	Water Chestnuts, drained and chopped
2 cups	Sour Cream
1 cup	Mayonnaise
1 teaspoon	Dried Dill Weed

Combine ingredients. Chill for at least one hour. Serve in bread bowl reserve bread for dipping, mini french toasts (recipe below), or water crackers.

Herbed French Croutons

1 loaf	Fresh French Bread
2 Tablespoons	Olive Oil
2 Tablespoons	Garlic Salt

Slice french bread in ¼ inch rounds. Brush with olive oil and dust with garlic salt. Bake at 300 degrees until lightly golden brown.

Tabbouleh

Yields 12 Servings

2 cups	Fresh Parsley
¼ cup	Onions, Finely Diced
1 cup	Tomatoes, Diced
1 cup	Cucumbers, pealed and diced
1 teaspoon	Fresh Mint
1 cup	Couscous
¼ cup	Lemon Juice
½ cup	Olive Oil
1 teaspoon	Fine Sea Salt
14 ounces	Pita Bread (pocket size)

Prepare Couscous per package directions. Stem and finely chop parsley. Combine first nine ingredients and mix well. Chill at least 1 hour. Warm Pita Bread in 200 degree oven for 10 minutes. Slice Pita Bread into pie shaped wedges. Serve pita bread with chilled Tabbouleh.

Spinach Gruyere Puff Pastry

Yields 12 Servings

1 Sheet	Puff Pastry (I recommend Pepperidge Farms)
10 ounce package	Frozen Chopped Spinach, thawed
4 tablespoons	Butter, divided
1 cup	Mushrooms, sliced
4 ounces	Gruyere Cheese
1/2 teaspoon	Fine Sea Salt
1 tablespoon	Garlic Salt

Drain spinach well, be sure to remove excess moisture with paper towels. Melt 2 Tablespoons butter in a skillet over medium heat. Add mushrooms and saute for 5 minutes. Stir in spinach, cheese and salt then set aside. Melt remaining 2 Tablespoons of butter and brush over the pastry. Spread spinach mixture on the top of puff pastry. Roll up like a jellyroll, starting with the long side. Wrap roll in plastic wrap and refrigerate at least 1 hour. Cut roll into 1/2 inch thick slices. Place on a parchment lined baking sheet. Dust with garlic salt. Bake for 15 to 20 minutes at 425 degrees, or until golden brown. You may substitute Gruyere cheese with Swiss or Mozzarella.

Crab Puff Pastry Triangles Page 59

APPETIZERS

Crab Puffs
Pastry Triangles

Yields 20 Servings

5	Puff Pastry Squares 5x5
1/4 teaspoon	Sea Salt
½ medium	Lemon - fresh squeezed juice
2 tablespoons	Lemon Zest
1/4 cup	Parsley - fresh snipped
1/8 cup	Paprika
2 ounces	Butter - melted

Crab Filling

2 ounces	Lemon Juice - fresh squeezed
8 ounces	Cream Cheese - softened
8 ounces	Crab Meat - drained
A pinch	Salt and Pepper
1/4 cup	Parsley - freshly snipped

Cut pastry square into triangles 4 per square. Place puff pastry triangles ¼ inches apart on a cookie sheet. Lightly baste with melted butter. Sprinkle sea salt, lemon juice, paprika, and parsley on each triangle. Bake at 450 degrees until lightly golden brown. Let cool for 20 minutes and separate each triangle in to two pieces, a top and a bottom. In a medium mixing bowl combine cream cheese, crab meat, lemon juice, parsley, salt, and pepper. Refrigerate mixture until you are ready to assemble. Place 1 tablespoon of crab mixture in each puff pasty triangle. Serve hot or cold. Garnish with lemon zest and finely chopped parsley.

APPETIZERS

Baked Brie Purses with Peach Chutney Voyant

Yields 8 Servings

8 5 x5 inch	Puff Pastry squares
(I recommend Pepperidge Farms)	
8 ounce	Brie wheel
1/2 cup	Peach jam
8 ounces	Peaches, frozen chunked
1/4 cup	Brandy
2 tablespoons	Salted butter
1/4 cup	Large pecan pieces

Cut a 1/2 inch strip from one side of each Pastry Square. Set the eight strips aside for the top decoration. Cut the chilled Brie wheel into eight pie shaped wedges. Place each of the one ounce Brie wedges in the middle of each pastry square. Bring all four pastry corners up, pinch the corners together at the top of pastry envelope. Repeat until all eight pieces of brie are in pastry envelopes. Take the remaining strips of pastry and cut the four corners off at an 45 degree angle. Twist the middle of each strip and place at the top of the pastry envelope and pinch the pastry forming the bow with the strip. Bake at 400 degrees for 15 minutes until golden brown. Place in small bread plate.

Combine the jam, peaches, brandy, butter and pecans in a small saute pan. Saute on low heat until the chutney is cooked to a honey color. Serve with chutney drizzled in top of the baked pastry purses.

Chicken Wings

Yields 12 Servings

12	Chicken Wings
1/2 cup	Soy Sauce
1/3 cup	Sugar
1/4 cup	Pineapple Juice
4 tablespoons	Oil
2 teaspoons	Garlic Powder
2 teaspoons	Ginger

Cut chicken wings apart, trim tips and discard. Makes 24 pieces. Combine soy sauce, sugar, pineapple juice, oil, garlic powder, and ginger. Add chicken pieces to mixture. Marinate covered overnight or for several hours. Bake at 350 degrees for 1 hour uncovered.

APPETIZERS

Fried Green Tomatoes

Yields 8 Servings

4	Large Green Tomatoes
2	Eggs
½ cup	Milk
1 cup	Flour
½ cup	Cornmeal
½ cup	Bread Crumbs
2 teaspoons	Salt
¼ teaspoons	Pepper
1 qt.	Corn Oil

Slice tomatoes ½ inch thick. Whisk eggs and milk. Mix cornmeal, bread crumbs, salt, and pepper. Dip the tomatoes in flour. Then dip in the egg mixture. Finally coat with cornmeal mixture. In a large skillet heat oil (about ½ inch in bottom of pan) over medium heat. Place tomatoes in hot oil browning evenly on each side. Serve with buttermilk Dressing.

SOUP
SALADS
SIDES

Farm Fresh Ingredients

Crab Bisque with Croûton

Yields 4-6 Servings

3 tablespoons	Butter
2-3	Onion, finely chopped
1 can	Crab Meat with Juice
2-3 teaspoons	Paprika
4-6 tablespoons	Tawny Port or Sherry
3 cups	Heavy Whipping Cream
1 tablespoon	Corn Starch
1/4 cup	Water
1/2 teaspoon	Lemon Zest
1	Fresh Lemon, juiced
	Salt and Pepper to taste
1 loaf	French Bread
1/2 cup	Olive Oil
1 teaspoon	Garlic Salt
1/4 cup	Parsley

In a medium sauce pan sauté butter, onion, crab (with juice), Paprika (to color), Port or Sherry, Add Heavy Whipping Cream, Corn Starch in water. Add a little Lemon Zest, fresh squeezed lemon and salt and pepper to taste. Bring to a boil and reduce heat and simmer until slightly thickened. Serve with Crouton. Cut French bread rounds (¼ to ½ " thick) with a pastry brush spread olive oil, sprinkle with garlic salt and parsley. Bake until golden brown.

French Onion Soup

Yields 6 Servings

4 cups	Yellow Onions, sliced in moons
4 tablespoon	Butter
1 tablespoon	Sugar
¼ Cup	Red Wine
5 Cups	Water
¼ Cup	Beef Base

Sauté yellow onions in butter and sugar until translucent. Add water, beef base, red wine. Bring to a boil and simmer over low heat. Serve with a crouton and top with mozzarella cheese and fresh parsley.

White Gazpacho

Yields 8 Servings

3 Large	Cucumbers
	Peeled, seeded, and chopped
2 Cloves	Garlic, minced
4-6 Little	Green Onions
2 cups	Water
1/3 cup	Olive Oil
2 teaspoons	Sea Salt
2 cups	Bread Crumbs, loosely packed
¼ cup	Vinegar
¼ cup	Lemon Juice
½ teaspoon	Chicken Base
¾ teaspoon	White Pepper

In a blender mix cucumbers, garlic, little green onions, water, sea salt, bread crumbs, vinegar, lemon juice, chicken base, and pepper. Additional seasonings to taste. Chill for at least 1 hour. Garnish with sour cream, diced cucumbers, tomatoes, onion, dill, and olive oil.

SOUP, SALADS & SIDES

Apple Salad (Vegan)

Yields 6 Servings

3 medium	Apples, diced
2 stalks	Celery, sliced
½ cup	Wheat Berries, cooked as directed
¼ cup	Raisins
¼ cup	Walnuts
1/3 cup	Veganaise
1/3 cup	Toufuti
2 teaspoons	Mint, chopped

In a small bowl mix the veganaise, and toufuti. Combine apples, celery, wheat berries, raisins, walnuts. Add veganaise mix. Stir in mint. Chill for one hour.

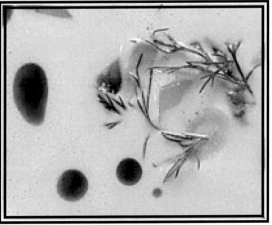

White Gazpacho Page 66

Linda's Bubble Salad

Yields 6 Servings

1 cup	Baby Pearl Tapioca
6 cups	Water
1 small package	Jell-O
1/2 cup	Sugar
1 cup	Cool Whip

Boil six cups of water. When boiling add 1 cup of baby pearl tapioca. Bring to a boil. Cover and turn off heat. Leave sit for one hour tapioca will look clear. Add one small box of Jell-O, stir well. Add 1/2 cup sugar, stir well. Cool for 2 to 3 hours. Stir in 1 cup of cool whip. Refrigerate for at least 1 hour.

SOUP, SALADS & SIDES

Caprese Salad

Yields 6 Servings

3-vine ripe large	Tomatoes - sliced
15 medium	Fresh Basil Leaves - ribboned
4 tablespoons	Aged Balsamic Vinegar
1/2 cup	Extra Virgin Olive Oil
1/4 teaspoon	Garlic Salt
1/4 teaspoon	Fine Grind Sea Salt
1/4 teaspoon	White Pepper
1-8oz pkg	Fresh Buffalo Mozzarella Cheese - sliced

On large platter arrange alternating slices of tomatoes, and Mozzarella Cheese. Cut basil in to ribbons. Sprinkle basil, garlic salt, sea salt, and white pepper on top. Combine balsamic vinegar and olive oil. Drizzle on top. Serve chilled.

Caprese Salad
shown with
Potato Casserole
Page 87

Chicken Salad

Yields 6 Servings

4 cups	Chicken, cooked and diced
1 cup	Celery, mooned
½ cup	Red Onion, diced
¼ cup	Parsley, snipped
2 cups	Mayonnaise
½ teaspoon	Celery Salt
	Salt and Pepper to taste

Combine all ingredients and mix well. Chill at least one hour.

Brown Derby Cobb Salad
Yields 4 Servings

1/2 head	Iceberg Lettuce
1/2 bunch	Watercress
1 small bunch	Curly Endive
1/2 head	Romaine
2 tablespoons	Minced Chives
1	Chicken Breast, cooked and diced
6 Strips	Bacon, cooked and diced
1	Avocado, peeled and diced
3	Hard Boiled Eggs, peeled and diced
1/2 cup	Roqueford Cheese, crumbled

Finely chop and mix watercress, endive and romaine. Arrange chives, tomatoes, chicken, bacon, avocado, eggs, and cheese in rows over the lettuce.

Dressing

1/4 cup	Water
1/4 cup	Red Wine Vinegar
1/4 cup	Sugar
1 teaspoon	Fresh Squeezed Lemon Juice
2 teaspoons	Salt
3/4 teaspoon	Fresh Ground Pepper
3/4 teaspoon	Worcestershire Sauce
1/4 teaspoon	Dry Mustard
1 clove	Garlic - minced
1 cup	Extra Virgin Olive Oil

Combine all ingredients mixing well. Chill for 1 hour. Drizzle over salad.

SOUP, SALADS & SIDES

The Best Egg Salad

Yields 4 Servings

6	Eggs, hard boiled, diced
¼ cup	Red Onion, diced
¼ cup	Celery, cut into crescent moons
¾ cup	Mayonnaise
½ teaspoon	Mustard
¼ teaspoon	Celery Salt
	Salt and pepper to taste

Combine all ingredients mixing well. Chill one hour. Serve on fresh bread.

Brown Derby Cobb Salad Page 71

Mediterranean Barley Salad

Yields 4 Servings

1 cup	Barley
2 1/2 cups	Water
7	Sun-dried Tomatoes, Sliced in Strips
2 cloves	Garlic, Minced
2 tablespoons	Olive Oil
1 tablespoon	Balsamic Vinegar
1/2 cups	Chopped Cilantro
1-4oz can	Black Olives, Sliced
1/2	Garlic Salt
1/4 cup	Chopped Sweet Bell Peppers
1/4 cup	Red Onion
	Roasted in Olive Oil and Garlic
1/3 Cup	Capers
2 teaspoon	Fresh Lemon Juice

Bring barley and water to a boil in a large pan. Reduce heat to low, cover, and simmer until barley is tender but, still firm. About 30 minutes. Drain and rinse with olive oil and cool to room temperature. In a small sauce pan roast garlic, and red onion in olive oil. Cook until translucent. Cool. Add sun-dried tomatoes, minced clove garlic, olive oil, garlic salt, balsamic vinegar, black olives, capers, cilantro, bell peppers, red onion, and lemon juice. Mix well. Chill well.

Potato Salad

Yields 12 Servings

5 pounds	Red Potatoes
6	Eggs, hard boiled, diced
½ cup	Red Onion, diced
1 cup	Celery, chopped into crescents
3 cups	Mayonnaise
3 tablespoons	Mustard
2 teaspoons	Salt
1 teaspoon	Pepper
2 teaspoons	Dill Weed
½ teaspoon	Celery Salt

Boil potatoes with skin on. Cool, and cut in to chunks. Add all ingredients mixing well. Chill. Garnish with fresh parsley.

View from the Observation Deck

Raspberry River House Salad

Yields 4 Servings

1 lb	Bacon - Cooked and crumpled
1 can	Mandarin Oranges - drained
1 small	Red Onion - sliced in rings
6 cups	Mixed Salad Greens

Glazed Pecans

2 cups	Pecans
1/2 cup	Maple Syrup
2 1/2 teaspoons	Worcestershire Sauce
1 tablespoon	Cinnamon
1 teaspoon	Vanilla
1/2 tablespoon	Brown Sugar

Combine all ingredients except the pecans into small bowl and mix well. Place pecans in a medium bowl and stir in glaze mixture. Spread mixture on a greased cookie sheet. Bake at 350 for 10 minutes. Remove and set aside. Combine Salad with Glazed Pecans and toss with Red Raspberry Vinaigrette dressing. Enjoy!

Victorian House Coleslaw

Yields 10 Servings

1 large	Head Cabbage
1 small	Head Red Cabbage
1/4 cup	Pecans
1 can	Mandarin Oranges, drained

Dressing

1 cup	Mayonnaise
1/3 cup	Sugar
1 tablespoon	Red Wine Vinegar

Julienne cabbage and place in to a large mixing bowl, set aside. In a small mixing bowl combine ingredients for the dressing, set aside. Add the dressing to the cabbage 1 hour before serving, refrigerate. Just before serving toss with Pecans and Oranges.

This is the slaw we have served at our luncheons for decades.

Cucumber-Basil Buttermilk Dressing

Yields 1 1/2 cups

1 clove	Garlic
2/3 cup	Buttermilk
1/3 cup	Light Mayonnaise
1/2	English Cucumber, cut in chunks
2 tablespoons	Chopped Fresh Basil or
	2 teaspoons dried basil
1 teaspoon	Dijon Mustard
1/4 teaspoon	Hot Pepper Sauce
1/3 cup	Low-fat Yogurt
Dash	Salt and Pepper

In a blender or food processor, process garlic, buttermilk, mayonnaise, cucumber, basil, mustard and hot pepper sauce until mixed. Stir in yogurt. Season with salt and pepper to taste. Cover and refrigerate (for 3 to 4 days).

Red Raspberry Vinaigrette

Yields 6 Cups

1/2 cup	Corn Syrup
2 cups	Oil
1/2 teaspoon	Garlic powder
1/2 teaspoon	Onion Salt
3/4 cup	Red wine vinegar
1/2 teaspoon	Pepper
1 cup	Water
1 pint	Frozen or Fresh Red Raspberries

Combine all ingredients into blender and mix/blend well.   Sweeten to taste if desired.

Balsamic Vinaigrette

Yields 6 Cups

¼ cup	Red Wine
½ cup	Balsamic Vinegar
½ teaspoon	Paprika
¼ cup	Parmesan Cheese, Grated
¾ cup	Swiss Cheese, Grated
¼ cup	Mozzarella Cheese, Grated
½ teaspoon	Basil
1 ½ Cups	Extra Virgin Olive Oil
½ teaspoon	Sea Salt
1 teaspoon	Pepper
1/3 cup	Garlic Cloves, Minced (about 6 cloves)
1 cup	Water
1 tablespoon	Sugar
2/3 Cup	Fresh Parsley, Chopped
2 teaspoon	Lemon Zest

Saute minced garlic in 1 tablespoon olive oil and cool   Mix all ingredients together. Chill at least 1 hour before serving.

French Dressing

Yields 3 Cups

1/2 cup	Sugar
1/3 cup	Catsup
3/4 cup	Vinegar
1/2	Lemon juice
1	Small Onion (grated)
1/2 tablespoon	Salt
1 cup	Oil

Mix all ingredients except oil together. Add oil, mix well. Blend all ingredients in blender until mixed well. Chill at least 1 hour before serving.

Mandarin Sesame Dressing

Yields 4 Cups

1 1/2 cups	Extra Virgin Olive Oil
1 1/2 cups	Water
1 can	Mandarin Oranges Juiced
1	Lemons (Juice)
1 teaspoons	Sesame Oil
1 cup	Sugar
1/4 teaspoon	Garlic
1 teaspoons	Ginger
1 teaspoons	Black Pepper
¼ cups	Sesame Seeds
1 teaspoon	Lemon Zest

Mix all ingredients together. Chill at least 1 hour before serving.

Mediterranean Dressing

Yields 4 Cups

2 Cups	Extra Virgin Olive Oil
1 ½ Cups	Water
½ Cup	Lemon Juice (Fresh Squeezed)
16 Cloves	Garlic, Minced
½ teaspoon	White Pepper
3 tablespoons	Sea Salt
1 teaspoon	Lemon Zest

Mix minced garlic, sea salt, and white pepper to form a paste. Add all other ingredients and mix well. Chill at least 1 hour before serving.

Sweet Potato Pie

Yields 6 -8 Servings

1 pound	Sweet Potatoes
	Boiled, peeled, and mashed
½ cup	Butter
1 cup	Brown Sugar
2	Eggs
½ teaspoon	Nutmeg

Mix all ingredients together and pour in to a 9" pie shell and bake at 350 degrees for one hour.

Vichy Carrots

Yields 6 Servings

2 cups	Fresh Baby Carrots
2 tablespoons	Butter
1/4 cup	Granulated Sugar
1/2 cup	Fresh Parsley, finely chopped

In a large saute pan melt butter. Add baby carrots and sugar. Cook until al dente. Turn off heat add parsley. Cover for 2 minutes. Turn out to heated casserole dish.

French Beans with
Shallots and Tarragon

Yields 4 Servings

1 lb	Green beans
2 cups	Water
2 tablespoons	Shallots, chopped
2 tablespoons	Butter
2 tablespoons	Tarragon, fresh chopped

In a large sauce pan bring water to boil. Add salt and beans. Bring to a boil and simmer for 8-10 minutes. Beans should be tender but crisp, drain. Sauté shallots in butter. Add green beans, tarragon, salt and pepper. Cook until al dente.

Oven Roasted Squash

Yields 4 Servings

2	Acorn Squash
6 tablespoons	Butter
1 1/3 cups	Brown Sugar
1 teaspoon	Cinnamon
1/2 teaspoon	Ground Clove
1 1/2 cups	Water

Wash and dry squash. Microwave whole squash for 10 minutes. Cut in half and remove seeds. Place 1 1/2 cups water in a 9x 13 pan. Place squash cut side in to pan. In each of the 4 squash cups place 2 tablespoons butter, 1/3 cup brown sugar. Sprinkle cinnamon and clove evenly in to each cup. Cover with foil. Bake at 350 degrees for 1 hour or until tender.

Potato Casserole

Yields 8-10 Servings

6 large	Potatoes, Boiled and sliced
¼ cup	Red Onions, mooned
½ stick	Butter
¼ cup	Oil
1 cup	Shredded Cheddar Cheese
1 cup	Sour Cream
½ cup	Half and Half or Heavy Cream
¼ cup	Parsley, snipped
1 teaspoon	Garlic Powder
½ teaspoon	Onion Powder
½ teaspoon	Poultry Seasoning
	Salt and Pepper to taste

Sauté onions in butter. Add oil, potatoes, garlic powder, onion powder, poultry seasoning, salt, and pepper. Cook for about 10 minutes. Place potatoes in to a large baking dish. In a small bowl mix sour cream and heavy cream, pour over potatoes and add parsley, cheese, mix well. Bake at 350 degrees for 25 minutes and garnish with parsley.

Ratatouille with Portabella Mushrooms

Yields 6 servings

1 pound	Yellow Squash
1 pound	Zucchini
1 pound	Egg Plant
1/2 medium	Red Onion
2	Garlic Cloves - Minced
1/2 cup	V-8 juice
1/4 cup	Olive Oil
2 large	Portabella Mushrooms
1 tablespoon	Butter
	Salt and Pepper to taste

Wash and dry all vegetables, cut zucchini, squash, onion in a large dice. Heat large skillet, add oil, and sauté onion lightly, add V-8 juice, squash, zucchini and salt and pepper to taste. Sauté until vegetables start to breakdown. Julienne the Portabella mushrooms. Melt butter in skillet; add mushrooms and salt and pepper. Sauté until just tender. Place on top of ratatouille and serve.

Rici E Bici

Yields 4 Servings

1/4 stick	Butter
1 cup	Rice
2 cups	Chicken Stick
1/4 cup	Red Onion, diced
1/4 teaspoon	Garlic Salt
1/4 teaspoon	White Pepper
1	Bay Leaf
1/4 cup	Frozen Peas

In a small sauce pan saute red onion in butter. Add 1/2 cup rice and brown. Add remaining rice, chicken stock, garlic salt, white pepper, and bay leaf. Cover and reduce heat to low. Do not stir. Simmer until water has boiled out. Approximately 15-20 minutes. Add frozen peas, cover for 5 minutes. Stir gently and serve.

Rici E Bici, Ginger Chicken, and Oven Roasted Squash

Southern Style Sweet Potatoes

Yields 6 -8 Servings

6 large	Sweet Potatoes
1 stick	Butter
1 cup	Brown Sugar
1 teaspoon	Cinnamon

Bake sweet potatoes at 375 degrees until soft. Peel. Add butter, brown sugar, cinnamon and mash well. Serve with pecan sauce.

Pecan Sauce

½ cup	Pecan Pieces
½ stick	Butter
½ cup	Water
¼ cup	Brandy
½ cup	Brown Sugar
½ tsp	Ground Cloves

In a small sauce pan toast pecans in butter. Add remaining ingredients and simmer over low heat.

ENTREES

Cappellini Di Mare Page 98

ENTREES

Chicken Chesapeake

Yields 4 Servings

4-8 oz	Lump Crabmeat
3-4 (2 lbs)	Boneless Skinless Chicken Breasts
4 tablespoons	Butter (salted), divided
1/2 cup	Minced Green Onions
1 cup	Dry White Wine
1 cup	Heavy Whipping Cream
1 cup	Chicken Broth
8 oz	Cream Cheese
1/2 teaspoon	Garlic powder
1/2 teaspoon	Old Bay Seasoning
	Salt and pepper to taste

Preheat oven to 350 degrees. Spray casserole dish with cooking spray. Sprinkle crabmeat evenly over the baking dish. Distribute 1-2 tbs of butter in slivers throughout bottom of the dish with crab. Season crab with salt, pepper, and Old Bay Seasoning.

Sprinkle chicken with salt & pepper, garlic powder, and Old Bay Seasoning. In a large skillet, melt 1-2 tbs butter over medium heat. Add wine and chicken. Saute 4-5 minutes per side or until golden brown. Place over crab.

Melt remaining butter in same skillet over medium heat. Add onions and wine. Cook until reduced by half. Stir in chicken broth and cream. Cook for 10 minutes or until slightly thickened. Add cream cheese, stir until melted. Season with salt, pepper, and garlic. Pour over chicken and bake for 25-30 minutes until hot and bubbly. Serve over cooked rice.

Chicken Vesuvio

Yields 4 Servings

6 medium	New Potatoes, quartered
4 (6 ounce)	Skinless, Boneless
	Chicken Breast Halves
2 teaspoons	Olive Oil
1/4 cup	Fresh Lemon Juice
2 teaspoons	Fresh Rosemary, minced
1 teaspoon	Minced Garlic
	Salt and Pepper to Taste
1/8 cup	Green onions, chopped
1/8 cup	Pitted black olives, sliced
1/2 cup	Mushrooms, sliced

Place potatoes and chicken in a casserole dish. Drizzle with olive oil and lemon juice. Then sprinkle with rosemary, garlic, salt, and pepper. Cover, and refrigerate for at least 30 minutes. Peheat oven to 400 degrees F (200 degrees C). Sprinkle green onions over chicken. Bake, covered, in preheated oven for 30 minutes. Remove, and add olives and mushrooms. Return to oven, and bake for 30 minutes. Transfer chicken and vegetables to platter, and pour pan juices on top.

ENTREES

Rock Cornish Game Hen

Yields 4 Servings

4	Game Hens - thawed and rinsed.
3 cups	Croutons for stuffing
1/2 cup	Onions, diced
1/2 cup	Celery, moons
4 ounces	Butter
1 cups	Chicken Stock
4 teaspoons	Currants

In a medium bowl put croutons, set aside. Sauté diced onions and celery moons in butter add chicken stock. Poor butter mixture over the croutons. Stir in well. Add currants 1 t. per hen. Add water to soften if needed. Place hens' legs up in a foiled pan. Butter the top of the hen, and cover loosely with foil. Baste regularly, starting after the first 1/2 hour. Bake at 350 degrees for 1 hour and 15 minutes.

Cumberland Sauce

1 jar	Currant Jelly
1 jar	Red Wine
1 teaspoon	Worcestershire Sauce
1 tablespoon	Butter
1 tablespoon	Cornstarch
1/4 cup	Warm Water

In a sauce pan over low heat combine current jelly, and red wine. Melt to a liquid. Add worcestershire sauce, and butter. Bring to a boil over medium high heat. Put 1 tablespoon corn starch in a small bowl and mix with water to form a paste. Add corn starch mixture to sauce, reduce heat to medium (Sauce should thicken after a few minutes if not add one teaspoon cornstarch and water).

ENTREES

Ginger Chicken

Yields 4 Servings

4-8 ounce	Chicken Breasts (skin on) thawed
2 -3 cups	Drake's Fry Mix
1/4 cup	Sesame Seeds
3 large	Eggs
1/4 cup	Milk
2 cups	Oil (to fry chicken)
1 can	Lemonade Concentrate
1 can	Water
1/2 cup	Soy Sauce
2 tablespoons	Corn Oil
	(reserve 2 T oil used to fry chicken)
1/2 cup	Green Onions
1/2 teaspoon	Ginger
1/2 cup	Sugar
1 tablespoon	Corn Starch

Preheat oven to 350F. Place chicken breasts into egg and milk mixture. Set aside. In a large bowl add Drake's Fry mix, and sesame seeds, mix together. Place chicken into the fry mixture, covering chicken completely, set a side. Put oil into a large frying pan, when hot, fry chicken until lightly browned, reserve 2 Tablespoons oil to saute onions in. Remove chicken from pan and place chicken into a foiled baking pan. Place 1 tablespoon sauce over each piece of chicken, cover with foil. Bake at 350F for 45 min. to 1 hour. After baking top each piece of chicken with 1 tablespoon of sauce.

Ginger Sauce

Sauté green onions in 2 tablespoons of the Oil, set a side. Mix corn starch with water, and lemonade, set a side. In a medium sauce pan combine, soy sauce, ginger, sugar, and green onions. Bring to a boil over medium heat and add corn starch mixture. Heat over medium until sauce begins to thicken.

Iowa Stuffed Pork Chop
with Lemon Caper Butter Wine Sauce

Yields 4 Servings

4 -2"	Center Cut Iowa Pork Chop (Bone in)
3 cups	Croutons for stuffing
1/2 cup	Onions
1/2 cup	Celery
4 ounces	Butter
1 cups	Chicken Stock
1/2 teaspoon	Sage

In a medium bowl put croutons, set aside. Sauté diced onions and celery moons in a stick of butter add chicken base, and sage. Poor the butter mixture over the croutons. Stir in well. Add water to soften if needed. Stuff the Chop with Sage Stuffing. Place stuffed chop in a foiled pan uncovered. Bake 350 degrees for about and 1 hour fifteen minutes. Serve with sauce and garnish with lemon twist.

Chop Sauce

1 stick	Butter
3 tablespoons	Capers
3 tablespoons	White Wine

Melt 1 stick of butter. Add 3 tablespoons of capers per 1 stick of butter. Add 3 tablespoons of white wine and stir over low heat.

Italian Beef Sandwiches

Yields 6 Servings

1 cup	Onion Soup
1 cup	Beef Broth
1 teaspoon	Oregano
2 cloves	Garlic, Minced
2 pounds	Chuck Roast
2 tablespoons	Butter
6	Hoggie Buns

Cook Chuck Roast with salt and pepper in a covered pan on stove top over medium heat until well done about 2 hours. You may need to add water if it begins to stick. Pull meat and add Onion Soup, Beef Broth, Oregano, and Garlic. Continue to simmer for 30 minutes. Brush hoggie buns with butter bake face up until lightly toasted. Remove beef from liquid and arrange on buns.

Capellini Di Mare

Yields 2 Servings

3 tablespoon	Butter
1/2 teaspoon	Minced Garlic
8 medium	Scallops
6 large	Shrimp Prawns
2 tablespoons	Lemon Juice fresh squeezed & zest
1/4 teaspoon	Salt
1/4 teaspoon	Pepper
1/4 teaspoon	Paprika
1/2 cup	Sliced Mushrooms
4 dashes	Tabasco Sauce
1 cup	Heavy cream
2 tablespoons	White cooking Sherry or Marsala Wine
1/4 cup	Romano Cheese or Parmesan Cheese
4-6	Roasted Red Peppers
8 oz	Angel Hair

In a medium sauce pan, place butter, minced garlic, scallops, shrimp, lemon juice, lemon zest, salt, pepper, and paprika. Cook for one minute and add sliced mushrooms. Cook until translucent. Add to dashes of tabasco sauce, heavy cream, white cooking sherry. Cook until the sauce begins to bubble at the edges. Remove from heat and add romano cheese, red peppers.

Boil angle hair in salted water with a teaspoon of olive oil. Cook 3-5 minutes or until al dente. Rinse with warm water. Toss with olive oil, and garlic salt. Arrange seafood in the center of pasta. Spoon sauce over seafood pasta. Garnish with fresh basil, oregano, parsley, romano cheese, capers, and a lemon wedge.

Pasta Primavera Page 102

Ginger Chicken, Rici E Bici, Oven Roasted Squash Pages 95, 89, 86

ENTREES

Pasta Alfredo

Yields 2 Servings

2 tablespoons	Butter
3/4 teaspoon	Minced Garlic
2 cups	Heavy Cream
1/4 cup	Freshly grated Parmesan cheese
	Salt to Taste
1/4 teaspoon	Freshly Ground Pepper
8 ounces	Fettuccine or Angel Hair, cooked

Sauté butter and garlic in a medium sauce pan. Whisk in cream, salt, pepper, and parmesan. To reduce sauce Heat over medium low heat. Garnish pasta with sautéed mushrooms in butter, salt, and pepper. And a mixture of mozzarella, parmesan, and parsley.

Rigatoni Di Gregorio

Yields 2 Servings

1 tablespoon	Extra Virgin Olive Oil
5 ounces	Button Mushrooms
½	Yellow Onion, Diced
1 tablespoon	Garlic Puree
	Salt and Pepper to taste
5 oz	Raw Chicken Breast, Cut in to 1 ½ inch pieces
1 pint	Chicken Stock
1 pint	Heavy Cream
2-4 ounces	Marsala Wine
1 ounces	White Wine
8 ounces	Rigatoni
½ tablespoon	Chopped Fresh Basil
½ tablespoon	Chopped Fresh Parsley
1 tablespoon	Fresh Parmesan Cheese
1 ounce	Garlic Butter

Heat oil. Saute mushrooms, onion, and garlic. Add chicken, stock, marsala, white wine, and season with salt and pepper. Cook until reduced by half. Add cream and bring to a boil. Reduce heat and simmer. Cook rigatoni al dente, rinse, and add to chicken mixture. Add fresh basil, parsley, parmesan cheese, garlic butter, and salt and pepper to taste. Garnish with Parmesan Cheese, and Fresh Parsley.

Pasta Primavera

Yields 4 Servings

8 oz	Mushrooms, sliced
1 small	Red Onion, 1/8" sliced rings
2 small	Zucchini Squash, 1/4" medallions
1 teaspoon	Fresh Garlic, minced
1 jar	Premium Prepared Pasta Sauce
1 large	Tomato, diced
1/4 cup	Red Wine
1/2 teaspoon	Oregano
1/2 teaspoon	Basil
1/8 teaspoon	Sea Salt
1/8 teaspoon	Freshly ground pepper
16 ounces	Fettuccine or Angel Hair, cooked

Sauté zucchini squash onions, mushrooms, garlic, basil, and oregano in olive oil. Salt and pepper to taste. Saute for 15 minutes on low heat. Add tomatoes, pasta suace, and wine to the vegetables. Simmer for 15 minutes. Arrange the noodles in a pasta bowl in a small ring. Spoon the vegetable sauce in the center of pasta. Garnish pasta with a mixture of mozzarella cheese, parmesan cheese, and parsley.

ENTREES

Tilapia with Mushroom Cream Sauce

Yields 2 -4 Servings

1/2 cup	Sliced Mushrooms
4 tablespoons	Butter
1/2 teaspoon	Salt
1/2 teaspoon	Pepper
1/2 teaspoon	Lemon Zest
2 teaspoons	Lemon Juice
4 filets	Tilapia
1/2 cup	Heavy Cream
2 tablespoons	White Wine

Sauté sliced mushrooms in butter over medium heat. Add salt, pepper, lemon zest, and fresh squeezed lemon juice. Sear Tilapia 1 to 2 minutes on each side add cream and 2 T white wine. Garnish with fresh chopped parsley and lemon zest.

Valentines Day at Mont Rest

DESSERTS

Easy Lemon Meringue Pie, French Vanilla Cappuchino, and Almond Biscotti

Pages 118, 34, 133

DESSERTS

Watergate Dessert

Yields 15 Servings

1 cup	Flour
1 cup	Pecans, chopped
8 tablespoons	Butter, softened
8 ounces	Cream Cheese, softened
1 cup	Powdered Sugar
2 small boxes	Pistachio Instant Pudding
2 2/3 cups	Milk

Mix flour, 1/2 cup pecans, and butter. Press in to a 9x13 pan. Bake at 350 degrees for 15 minutes or until lightly browned. Set a side until cool.

Whipped Cream Topping

1 quart	Heavy Cream
3/4 cup	Sugar
1 teaspoon	Vanilla

Whip heavy cream on high until soft peaks form. Slowly add sugar and vanilla extract.

Filling

Mix cream cheese and powdered sugar. Add half of the whipped cream topping, mixing well. Spread on to cooled crust. Mix pudding and milk for 3 minutes. Spread on top of cream cheese layer. Spread on remaining whipped cram topping. Sprinkle with rest of chopped pecans. Chill for 3 hours.

Tres Leches Cake (3 Milk Cake)

Yields 2 Servings

1 cup	Sugar, divided
5	Eggs separated
5	Egg Whites
1/3 cup	Milk
1 teaspoon	Pure Vanilla Extract, divided
1 cup	Flour (all-purpose)
1 1/2 teaspoon	Baking Powder
1 can (14 oz)	Sweetened Condensed Milk
1 can (12 oz)	Evaporated Milk
1 Pint	Heavy Cream

Preheat oven to 350 degrees. Butter and Flour Pan. You may use a 9 inch springform or 8 x 12 inch pan. Beat egg yolks and 3/4 cup sugar until light in color and about double the volume. Add milk, vanilla, flour, and baking powder, mix well. In a medium bowl, beat egg whites until peaks form. Gradually add 1/4 cup sugar. Fold egg whites in to yolk mixture. Pour in prepared pan and bake about 20 - 35 minutes or until done. Allow to cool for 10 - 15 minutes and remove from pan.

Place on a large serving dish or decorative pan, completely cool the cake. Pierce cake with a meat fork. Mix sweetened condensed milk, evaporated milk, and 1/4 cup of heavy cream, slowly pour mixture over cake until it is absorbed. Refrigerate for 1 - 2 hours. Separately whip 5 egg whites and sugar (just like meringue) and Whip heavy cream, sugar, and vanilla. Stir together and frost cake. Drizzle homemade caramel sauce (page 124) and enjoy!

DESSERTS

Strawberry Rhubarb Pie

Yields 6-8 Servings

2	Pie shells (rolls onto pastry mat)
1 1/4 cups	Sugar
1/3 cup	Flour
2 cups	Rhubarb
2 cups	Strawberries - sliced
2 tablespoons	Butter
1 large	Egg

Stir together sugar and flour. Place 1 cup rhubarb and 1 cup strawberries into pie shell. Sprinkle 1/2 of the flour and sugar mix and repeat with remaining ingredients. Dot with butter and cover with top crust, seal and flute. Brush top with 1 beaten egg white and sprinkle with sugar and cut slits into top. Bake at 400 degrees for 40 to 50 minutes.

Rhubarb Upside Down Cake

Yields 4-6 Servings

1/2 cup	Sugar
1 large	Egg
1/4 cup	Butter
1/2 cup	Milk
1/2 teaspoon	Salt
1 cup	Flour
3 teaspoon	Baking Powder
2 cups	Rhubarb (cut into small pieces)
1 teaspoon	Nutmeg (for garnish)

Grease a 8x8 pan, place rhubarb in bottom of pan, set aside. Mix sugar, eggs, butter, milk, salt, flour, and baking powder together well. Pour mixture over rhubarb and bake at 400 for 30 to 40 minutes. Turn upside down on to serving platter. Serve with milk or cream and garnish with nutmeg.

DESSERTS

Rhubarb Custard Pie

Yields 6-8 Servings

1	9-inch pie shell
4 teaspoons	Flour
3 1/2 cups	Chopped Rhubarb
1 1/2 cups	Sugar
3 large	Eggs - beaten
1/8 teaspoon	Salt
1/4 cup	Light Cream

Sprinkle 1 teaspoon of the flour on crust, set aside. Mix all ingredients together including the rest of the flour. Pour into pie shell and bake 375 degrees for 1 hour.

DESSERTS

Pumpkin Streusel Pie

Yields 6-8 Servings

Streusel Topping

1/4 cup	Brown Sugar
2 tablespoons	Flour
2 tablespoons	Margarine
1/2 cup	Pecans

Pumpkin Mixture

1	9 inch pie shell
1/2 cup	Sugar
2 cups	Pumpkin
1 1/2 cups	Evaporated Milk
1 1/2 teaspoons	Pumpkin Pie Spice
2	Eggs, beaten

Mix all ingredients for streusel topping well and set aside. Next beat all ingredients for pumpkin mixture until mixed well and pour into a 9-inch pie shell Bake at 425 degrees for 15 minutes. Reduce heat to 350 degrees for 15 minutes. Sprinkle streusel topping on top and bake 15-20 minutes until done.

DESSERTS

Pecan Pie

Yields 6-8 Servings

3 large	Eggs
2/3 cup	Sugar
1 cup	Pecans
1/3 cup	Melted Butter
1 cup	Corn Syrup
1/2 teaspoon	Salt
1 teaspoon	Vanilla
1	9 Inch Pie Shell

Beat eggs sugar, salt, butter, and corn syrup until well mixed. Stir in vanilla and pecans. Pour in to pie shell and bake at 375 degrees for 40 to 50 minutes or until well set.

DESSERTS

Peach Pie

Yields 6-8 Servings

2 crust	9-inch Pie Shell
5 cups	Fresh Peaches - sliced
1 teaspoon	Lemon Juice
1 cup	Sugar
1/4 cup	Flour
1/4 teaspoon	Cinnamon
2 tablespoon	Butter

In a large bowl mix peaches and lemon juice. In a small bowl stir together sugar, flour, and cinnamon. Mix cinnamon and sugar mixture with peaches, turn into pie shell. Dot with butter and cover with top crust, seal and flute. In a small bowl beat 1 egg white and 1 T. water, brush top of pie. Bake 425 degrees for 35 to 45 minutes or until crust is brown and juice begins to bubble out.

Cheesecake Page 116

Homemade Pies

DESSERTS

New York-Style Cheesecake

Yields 10-12 Servings

Vanilla Wafer Crust

1 3/4 cups	Finely crushed vanilla wafers
1/2 cup	Butter, melted

In a small bowl stir together crushed wafers and melted butter. Stir until well combined. Press crumb mixture evenly into the bottom and up the sides of a greased 9-inch springform pan. Set aside.

New York Filling

32 oz	Cream Cheese
1 cup	Sugar
3 tablespoons	Flour
5	Eggs
1/3 cup	Whipping Cream
1 teaspoon	Finely shredded Orange peel
1 teaspoon	Finely shredded Lemon peel
1 teaspoon	Vanilla Extract

In a small bowl combine cream cheese, 1 cup sugar, and flour. Beat with electric mixer until smooth. Add eggs, one at a time, beating well after each addition. Stir in whipping cream, orange peel, lemon peel, and 1 teaspoon vanilla extract. Pour cream cheese mixture over the crust. Bake at 350 degrees for 15 minutes. Lower the temperature to 200 degrees and bake for 1 hour and 20 minutes, or until the center no longer looks wet or shiny. Remove the cake from the oven. Stir together 1 cup sour cream, 2 Tablespoons sugar, and 1/2 teaspoon vanilla extract. Spread over warm cheesecake. Return cheesecake to the oven and bake for 15 minutes more. Remove from oven and run a knife around the inside edge of the pan. Do not chill cheesecake.

DESSERTS

Mont Rest Key Lime Pie

Yields 8 Servings

1 8 oz pkg.	Cream Cheese (softened)
1 can	Sweetened Condensed Milk
2/3 cup	Cold Water
3	Egg Yolks (beaten)
1/8 teaspoon	Salt
1/2 cup	Flour
5 tablespoons	Rose's Sweetened Lime Juice
5 tablespoons	Key Lime Juice
	or Reconstituted Lime Juice
1 teaspoon	Lime Zest (very fine)
1	Graham Cracker Pie Shell

Beat cream cheese until light and fluffy add sweetened condensed milk, beat mixture until completely blended. Use a 2 quart pan to whisk egg yolks with water, add salt and flour. Stirring constantly, completely mix flour into the liquid. Add lime zest, Rose's Lime Juice and Key Lime juice. On low heat, whisk the egg mixture and stir constantly until the mixture thickens resembling pudding in texture and thickness. When egg and flour mixture is thickened add cream cheese. Whisk constantly being very careful not to scorch the bottom of the pan. Stir until pie filling starts to thicken and is completely mixed. When pie filling is thick pour into the prepared pie shell. Chill pie for several hour before serving.

DESSERTS

Easy Lemon Meringue Pie

Yields 6-8 Servings

1	9-inch Pre baked Pie Crust
1 small	Lemon Jello Cook and Serve Pie Filling
2 large	Egg Yolks, beaten
½ cup	Sugar
¼ cup	Fresh Lemon Juice
2 cups	Water

In a medium sauce pan whisk together egg yolks, sugar and water. Cook over medium heat, stirring constantly, until thick.. Remove from heat, stir lemon juice and lemon zest, pour into crust.

Meringue

5 large	Egg Whites
1/2 cup	Sugar

Beat egg whites at medium speed until soft peaks form. Gradually beat in sugar at high speed until stiff peaks form. Spoon onto pie, covering edges. Bake at 350 degrees for 12 to 15 minutes or until golden.

DESSERTS

Cream Puffs

Yields 12 Servings

1 cup	Water
½ cup	Butter
1 cup	Flour, sifted
¼ teaspoon	Salt
4 large	Eggs

Preheat oven to 450 degrees. In a medium saucepan, melt butter and add water, bring to a boil. Add flour and salt all at once and stir until mixture forms a ball. It will look like mashed potatoes. Remove from heat and stir in eggs one at a time, stirring after each egg until smooth. Drop by teaspoon, 3 inches apart on a greased baking sheet. Bake 15 minutes and reduce heat to 325 degrees and bake an additional 25 minutes. Let cool and split each puff. Fill shells with whipped cream (page 120) and refrigerate or freeze. When ready to serve dust with powdered sugar and drizzle with melted chocolate sauce.

Custard Filling

2 tablespoons	Butter
¾ cup	Sugar
2 cups	Milk
1 teaspoon	Vanilla
¼ cup	Corn Starch
½ teaspoon	Salt
2 large	Egg yolks, beaten

Melt butter, add sugar, cornstarch and salt. Slowly add milk. Heat until boiling. Add egg yolks and cook for about 2 minutes. Remove from heat and add vanilla. Chill custard for at least 2 hours and pipe into shells.

DESSERTS

Coconut Cream Pie

Yields 6-8 Servings

1	9-inch Pre baked Pie Crust
4 1/3 cup	Milk, divided
1 cup	Sugar
2 teaspoons	Vanilla
3 tablespoons	Butter
½ cup, 1 tablespoon	Cornstarch
2 cups, 1 tablespoon	Coconut, toasted
2 cups	Whipped Cream

In a small bowl whisk cornstarch and 1/3 milk, set a side. In a medium sauce pan over medium heat bring rest of milk and sugar to a boil, stirring constantly. Add cornstarch mixture. Heat until thick stirring constantly. Remove from heat, stir in butter, vanilla, and 2 cups toasted coconut. Pour in to cooled shell. Refrigerate for 3 hours. Garnish with whipped cream and toasted coconut.

Whipped Cream

1 pint	Heavy Cream
½ cup	Sugar
1 teaspoon	Vanilla

In a large mixing bowl whip cream until it forms soft peaks, add sugar and vanilla slowly, until stiff peaks form.

DESSERTS

Chocolate Mousse

Yields 4 Servings

2 Squares (1 oz each)	Semisweet Chocolate, chopped
1 Square (1 oz)	Unsweetened Chocolate, chopped
3 tablespoons	Brandy, dark rum, or strong coffee
2 large	Eggs
1/3 cup	Sugar
1/8 teaspoon	Salt
2/3 cup	Heavy Cream
1 cup sweetened	Whipped Cream (for garnish)

In small heavy saucepan over low heat, melt chocolates with the brandy. Stir until smooth; set aside. In a small bowl, beat eggs, sugar, and salt until fluffy. Add cream; beat until mixture mounds slightly. Beat in chocolate mixture until well blended. Spoon into serving bowl. Chill Garnish with whipped cream.

Blender method: In blender, whirl eggs, sugar and salt 45 seconds or until frothy. Add cream and blend 10 seconds. Add chocolate mixture, blend until smooth. Proceed as above.

Featuring
Cream Puff
Page 119

DESSERTS

Bread Pudding

Yields 15 Servings

10 Slices	Dried White Bread, cubed
1/4 Cup	Butter, melted
2 teaspoon	Cinnamon
6 large	Eggs
3/4 cup	Granulated Sugar
2 teaspoon	Vanilla
1/2 teaspoon	Salt
3 cups	Hot Milk
1 pinch	Nutmeg

In a large mixing bowl combine bread, butter, and cinnamon, mix well. Transfer bread mixture into a lightly greased 2 quart baking dish. Using the same bowl beat eggs, sugar, vanilla, and salt, set a side. Add hot milk to egg mixture, mix well. Pour over bread cubes and sprinkle with nutmeg. Let bread soak for 5 minutes. Bake at 350 degrees for 30 minutes, or until knife inserted into the center comes out clean.

SAUCE

1/4 cup	Butter, melted
2 cup	Brown sugar
1/2 cup	Orange juice
1/8 cup	Brandy
1 teaspoon	Vanilla

Add orange juice to melted butter in saucepan. Blend in brown sugar and brandy. Mix well. Bring to boil and reduce heat to simmer. Cook until mixture coats spoon. Remove from heat and stir in vanilla. Cool and spoon over bread pudding. Garnish with whipped cream.

DESSERTS

Chocolate Cheesecake

Yields 10-12 Servings

Chocolate Cookie Crust

7 ounces	Chocolate Cookies (crushed)
6 tablespoons	Butter (melted)

Preheat oven to 350 degrees. Lightly grease base and sides of 9 in spring form pan. Mix chocolate cookie crumbs with butter. Press evenly into the bottom of spring form pan, Set aside.

Chocolate Filling

10 ounces	Unsweetened Chocolate (chopped into small pieces)
32 ounces	Cream Cheese (softened)
1 1/2 cups	Sugar
2 tablespoons	Vanilla
4	Eggs (room temperature)
3/4 cup	Sour Cream
1 tablespoon	Cocoa Powder

Melt chocolate pieces in microwave and set aside. Beat cream cheese until smooth, beat in sugar and vanilla. Add eggs one at a time beating well after each one. In a large bowl stir sour cream and cocoa powder to form a paste, set aside. Add cream cheese mixture to the chocolate mixture. Stir in melted chocolate and mix well until smooth. Pour mixture into crust and Bake 15 minutes at 350 degrees. Reduce heat to 225 degrees and bake 1 hour or until done.

DESSERTS

Elaine's Butterscotch Torte

Yields 10 Servings

6 large	Eggs, separated
1 1/2 cups	Sugar
1 teaspoon	Baking Powder
2 teaspoons	Vanilla
1 teaspoon	Almond Extract
2 cups	Graham Cracker Crumbs
1 cup	Nuts, chopped

Beat egg yolks well, slowly adding sugar, then baking powder and flavoring. Mix well. Beat egg whites until they hold stiff peaks, Fold in yolk mixture, crumbs, and nuts. Bake in a slow oven (325) for 30-35 minutes.

SAUCE

1/4 cup	Butter, melted
2 cup	Brown sugar
1/2 cup	Orange juice
1/8 cup	Brandy
1 teaspoon	Vanilla

Add orange juice to melted butter in saucepan. Blend in brown sugar and brandy. Mix well. Bring to boil and reduce heat to simmer. Cook until mixture coats spoon. Remove from heat and stir in vanilla. Cool and spoon over slices of torte.

DESSERTS

Bavarian Apple Torte

Yields 8-10 Servings

Crust

1/2 cup	Butter
1 1/4 cups	Flour
1/3 cup	Sugar
1/4 teaspoon	Vanilla extract

Filling

1 (8 oz.) package	Cream cheese
1/4 cup	Sugar
2 large	Eggs
1/2 teaspoon	Vanilla extract

Topping

4 cups	Sliced Apples with Peal
1 - 2 teaspoon	Cinnamon
1/3 cup	Sugar
1/3 cup	Apricot preserves
2 tablespoons	Water

In a mixing bowl, combine the butter, flour, sugar and vanilla until well blended. Pat into the bottom of a 10 inch springform pan. Bake in a preheated 400 degree oven for 5 - 10 minutes. Cool 5 minutes. Cook apple slices in sugar and cinnamon, set aside. In medium mixing bowl combine cream cheese, eggs, sugar and vanilla. Mix well. Pour into partially cooled crust. Arrange apples on top of cheese filling. Bake in 400 degree oven for 25 – 35 minutes. Cool. When cool, melt apricot preserves with a little water and brush over the top of the torte to give it a high glaze. Enjoy!

Apple Spice Cake

Yields 15 Servings

4 cups	Baking Mix (like Jiffy Mix)
1 cup	Flour
1 teaspoon	Baking Powder
1 ½ cup	Brown Sugar
1 cup, 1/4 cup	Granulated Sugar
3 large	Eggs
1 ½ cups	Milk
1 ½ sticks	Butter, melted
½ teaspoon	Ginger
1 teaspoon	Nutmeg
3 - 4 teaspoons	Cinnamon
4 cups	Sliced Apples

In a medium pan, sauté apples with ¼ cup sugar, 2-3 teaspoons cinnamon or to taste. In a medium bowl baking mix, flour, baking powder, ginger, nutmeg, cinnamon, set a side. In a medium bowl mix sugars, eggs, milk, and butter. Stir in dry ingredients. Mix well. Place batter in a greased 9x13 pan, add apples and top with brown sugar, cinnamon, and nutmeg. Bake 350 degrees, 1 hour or until done.

DESSERTS

Apple Pie

Yields 6-8 Servings

2	9-inch Pie Shells
6 cups	Thinly Sliced Tart Apples
3/4 cup	Sugar
1/4 cup	Flour
1/2 teaspoon	Nutmeg
1/2 teaspoon	Cinnamon
2 tablespoon	Butter
Dash of	Salt

Stir together sugar, flour, nutmeg, cinnamon, and salt. Mix in apples. Turn mixture into pie shell and dot with butter. Cover with top crust, seal and flute, cut slits in top. In a small bowl beat 1 egg white and 1 tablespoon water, brush on top of pie. Bake at 425 degrees for 40 to 50 minutes or until golden brown and juice begins to bubble out.

Trio of Desserts including Chocolate Mousse and

Chocolate Amaretto Ice Cream Crepes Pages 128, 121

DESSERTS

Amaretto Ice Cream Crepes with Chocolate Sauce

Yields 6-8 Servings

Shells

1 cup	Flour
2 tablespoons	Melted Butter
2 tablespoons	Granulated Sugar
1/3 cup	Milk
1 large	Egg
1 teaspoon	Real Vanilla
1 1/2 gallon	Ice Cream

Combine all ingredients in a medium bowl. Whisk well. Heat crepe pan over medium heat. Grease with butter. Spoon approximately 3 tablespoons of batter in to center of the pan. Rotate pan in a circle to form a french pancake. Cook 1-2 minutes on each side until golden brown. Fill with ice cream and serve with home made chocolate sauce. Garnish with whipped cream and chocolate shavings.

Chocolate Sauce

1/2 cup	Amaretto
2 cups	Dark Chocolate Pieces
1 cup	Heavy cream
1 teaspoon	Madagascar Vanilla Extract

Combine all ingredients in the top of a double boiler sauce pan. Stir over low heat until completely smooth and creamy. Pour over everything!!!

CANDIES
&
COOKIES

Gourmet Truffles

CANDIES & COOKIES

Chocolate Tuxedo Dipped Strawberries

Yields 12 Servings

12 large	Ripened Strawberries
3 ounces	Premium White Chocolate Pieces
3 ounces	Premium Almond Bark Pieces
10 ounces	Premium Dark Chocolate Pieces

Rinse Strawberries under running cold water but do not remove stems, be sure to pat strawberries completely dry with paper towels. Set strawberries aside.

Into double-broiler top (not over water) grate premium white chocolate pieces and premium almond bark pieces, heat over low until melted. Into a double-broiler top (not over water) grate premium milk chocolate pieces, heat until melted. Dip strawberries 3/4 the way up, place onto parchment, waxed, or lightly coated cookie sheet. Allow dipped strawberries to dry completely. Then dip strawberries into milk chocolate, one side at a time to form a V. Allow to dry. To make the bow tie and buttons; first pipe milk chocolate on the strawberry, into the shape of an X and fill in sides. Then add little dots of milk chocolate to form the buttons.

CANDIES & COOKIES

Gourmet Truffles

Yields 36 Servings

3 ½ Cups	Semisweet-chocolate pieces
1 Can	Sweetened Condensed Milk
¼ - 1/3 Cup	Brandy or your favorite Liquor

In double boiler over hot, not boiling, water (or in heavy, 2 quart saucepan over low heat), melt chocolate pieces. Stir in condensed milk, vanilla/liquor until well mixed. Refrigerate mixture overnight or 6 hours / until easy to shape. To melt in the microwave set power to 50% melt for 2 to 3 minutes. Stirring every 30 seconds. Shape mixture into 1 inch balls. Dip in melted chocolate or roll into cocoa or coconut.

Variations

Amaretto Truffles ~ use ¼ Cup Amaretto, 2 T. Brandy, 1 t. Vanilla. En-robe fondant in semi sweet chocolate coating. Garnish with a sliced Almond.

Bailey's Irish Cream Truffles ~ use white chocolate pieces in place of the semi- sweet, 1/3 cup Irish Cream Liquor. Roll fondant in chopped pecans and en-robe fondant in milk chocolate coating. Garnish with Chocolate Drizzle.

Homemade Vanilla Caramels

Yields 36 Servings

2 cups	Granulated Sugar
2 cups	Light Corn Syrup
8 tablespoons	Butter
1 cup	Half and Half
1 cup	Whipping Cream
1 teaspoon	Real Vanilla

In a large heavy pan add sugar, corn syrup, butter, and 1 cup half and half. Dissolve over low heat stirring constantly, until mixture comes to a boil. Cook over medium heat, stirring constantly, until just under the firm ball stage, 240 F. Add 1 cup whipping cream and cook to firm ball stage, 244 – 246. Remove from heat and add vanilla. Immediately pour caramel into a greased 7 ½ x 11 pan. Let cool overnight.

Hand Dipped Truffles and Caramels

Almond Espresso Biscotti

Yields 12 Servings

2 cups	Flour
1 cup	Sugar
½ teaspoon	Baking Soda
½ teaspoon	Baking Powder
½ teaspoon	Salt
½ teaspoon	Cinnamon
½ teaspoon	Ground Cloves
1 large	Egg Yolk
½ cup	Espresso or very Strong Coffee
1 tablespoon	Milk
1 teaspoon	Vanilla
1 cup	Almond Slices, toasted

Preheat oven to 350 degrees. Grease baking sheet. Mix, flour, sugar, baking soda, baking powder, salt, cinnamon, ground cloves. In a small bowl whisk egg yolk, chilled espresso, milk, and vanilla. Add to flour mixture. Mix until dough is formed. Add ¾ cup toasted almonds and mix by hand. Divide dough in half and place on cookie sheets to form a flattened log (rectangle). Make sides as straight and smooth as possible. Top with remaining ¼ cup toasted almonds. Bake until lightly browned, about 10 minutes. Let cool for 10 minutes and using a serrated bread knife cut in to 1 inch pieces. Reduce oven to 300 and place pieces back on cookie sheet and bake 10 minutes and turn pieces over. Turn oven off and leave in oven about a ½ hour. When completely cooled you may chocolate dip if desired.

Cherry Pecan Oatmeal Cookies

Yields 2 Dozen

1 cup	Granulated Sugar
1 cup	Brown Sugar
1 cup	Butter
2 large	Eggs
1 teaspoon	Vanilla
3 cups	Old fashioned oatmeal
2 cups	Flour
1/2 teaspoon	Salt
1 teaspoon	Baking Soda
1 teaspoon	Baking Powder
1 cup	Chopped Pecans
1 cup	Dried Cherries or Craisins

Beat sugar and butter until light and fluffy. Beat in eggs and vanilla. Combine dry ingredients and stir in by hand ingredients. Bake 8-10 minutes at 350 degrees.

CANDIES & COOKIES

Chocolate Chip Cookies

Yields 2 Dozen

1 cup	Butter
3/4 cup	Sugar
3/4 cup	Brown Sugar
2 large	Eggs
1 teaspoon	Vanilla
2 1/2 cups	Flour
1 teaspoon	Baking Soda
2 cups	Chocolate Chips

Mix sugars and butter together, add eggs and vanilla, mix well. Stir in flour and baking soda, add chocolate chips. Bake 350 degrees for 10 minutes.

Chocolate Crinkle Cookies

Yields 2 Dozen

1 cup	Unsweetened Cocoa Powder
2 cups	Granulated Sugar
½ cup	Vegetable Oil
4 large	Eggs
2 teaspoons	Vanilla
2 cups	Flour
2 teaspoons	Baking Powder
½ cup	Powdered Sugar

Mix cocoa, oil, and granulated sugar together, add eggs one at a time, mixing well after each egg. Stir in vanilla. Stir in flour and baking powder in to the cocoa mixture. Cover and chill for 4 hours. Roll into 1 ½ balls dip in powdered sugar. Bake 350 degrees for 10 -12 minutes.

CANDIES & COOKIES

Coconut Macaroons

Yields 20 to 22 Cookies

14 ounces	Sweetened shredded coconut
14 ounces	Sweetened condensed milk
1 teaspoon	Pure vanilla extract
2 extra-large	Egg whites, at room temperature
1/4 teaspoon	Kosher salt

Preheat the oven to 325 degrees F. Combine the coconut, condensed milk, and vanilla in a large bowl. Whip the egg whites and salt on high speed in the bowl of an electric mixer fitted with the whisk attachment until they make medium-firm peaks. Carefully fold the egg whites into the coconut mixture. Drop the batter onto sheet pans lined with parchment paper using either a 1 3/4-inch diameter ice cream scoop, or 2 teaspoons. Bake for 25 to 30 minutes, until golden brown. Cool and serve.

Momma's Oatmeal Cookies

Yields 2 Dozen

1 cup	Lard
1 cup	Sugar (heaping)
2 large	Eggs
6 tablespoons	Heavy Whipping Cream
1 teaspoon	Baking Soda
3 teaspoons	Cinnamon
2 cups	Oatmeal
2 cups	Flour
1 cup	Raisins

In a large mixing bowl mix lard and sugar together well. Stir in eggs and heavy whipping cream. Add baking soda, cinnamon, oatmeal, and flour. Stir well. Stir in raisins. Drop on cookie sheet. Bake at 375 degrees for 11 minutes.

CANDIES & COOKIES

Mont Rest Tea Time Pecan Tassies

Yields 2 Dozen

Ingredients for Crust

½ cup	Butter - softened
3 ounces	Cream Cheese - softened
1 cup	Flour

In a large bowl mix butter and cream cheese until well blended. Stir in flour. Firmly press mixture into a ball and refrigerate for 1 hour. Press evenly into bottom and sides of miniature muffin pan cups. Preheat oven to 350.

Ingredients for filling

2 large	Eggs
½ cup	Brown Sugar
½ cup	Corn Syrup
1 tablespoon	Melted Butter
½ teaspoon	Vanilla
1 cup	Chopped Pecans

In a medium bowl slightly beat egg. Stir in butter, brown sugar, and vanilla. Spoon 1 teaspoon of pecans in to each pastry lined cup. Spoon 1 Tablespoon of mixture on top of pecans. Bake 20 to 25 minutes or until lightly browned and toothpick comes out clean. Cool in pan 5 minutes. Sprinkle with confectioner's sugar and enjoy with your favorite cup of tea.

Peanut Butter Cookies

Yields 2 Dozen

1 cup	Shortening
1 cup	Sugar
1 cup	Brown Sugar
1 cup	Peanut Butter
2 large	Eggs, beaten
3 cups	Flour
2 teaspoons	Baking Soda
1 teaspoon	Vanilla

Mix all ingredients together, drop by spoon onto cookie sheet. Flatten with sugar dipped fork. Bake at 350 degrees for 10 minutes.

Every well dressed strawberry needs its own chocolate tuxedo.

CANDIES & COOKIES

Sparkling Sugar Cookies

Yields 2 Dozen

1/2 cup	Butter
1/2 cup	Shortening
1/2 cup	Sugar
1/2 cup	Powdered Sugar
1/2 teaspoon	Baking Soda
1/2 teaspoon	Cream of Tartar
1/8 teaspoon	Salt
1 large	Egg
1/2 teaspoon	Vanilla
2 cups	Flour

In a large mixing bowl, cream butter and shortening for 30 seconds. Add sugars, baking soda, cream of tartar, and salt until mixed well. Add egg and vanilla, mix well. Mix in flour as much as you can with the mixer. Stir in any remaining flour. Cover and chill for 3 hours. Shape cookies into 1 inch balls. Roll balls in granulated sugar and place three inches apart on an ungreased cooking sheet. Flatten into 2 ½ inch rounds using the bottom of a glass dipped in sugar. Bake at 350 degrees for 7 to 9 minutes or until lightly brown. Serve with icing and sprinkles or plain.

INDEX

INDEX

INDEX